Mediterranean Crock Pot Cookbook for Beginners

2000 Days of Slow Cooker Recipes, Easy, Delicious, and Budget-Friendly Meals for Quick and Convenient Meals

Zasper Vuxley

Table of Contents

INTRODUCTION

What is Mediterranean Cuisine?

Mediterranean cuisine is a diverse and flavorful culinary tradition that originates from the countries surrounding the Mediterranean Sea. This region, often referred to as the Mediterranean Basin, includes countries such as Greece, Italy, Spain, Turkey, Lebanon, and Morocco, among others. The cuisine of the Mediterranean is characterized by its emphasis on fresh, seasonal ingredients, olive oil, and an abundance of herbs and spices.

One of the defining features of Mediterranean cuisine is its focus on a balanced and healthy diet. The Mediterranean Diet, recognized for its potential health benefits, is centered around the consumption of fruits, vegetables, whole grains, legumes, nuts, and seeds. Olive oil, a staple in this diet, is rich in monounsaturated fats and is often used as the primary source of fat. Fish and seafood are also prominent components, providing a source of lean protein and omega-3 fatty acids.

Herbs and spices play a crucial role in Mediterranean cooking, adding depth and complexity to dishes. Common herbs include basil, oregano, thyme,

and rosemary, while spices such as cumin, coriander, and paprika are frequently used. The use of garlic and onions is prevalent, contributing to the bold flavors that characterize Mediterranean cuisine.

The Mediterranean region's diverse geography and climate influence the availability of ingredients, leading to regional variations in culinary traditions. For instance, Greek cuisine is known for its use of lamb, feta cheese, and yogurt, while Italian cuisine showcases pasta, tomatoes, and olive oil. Spanish cuisine is famous for paella, tapas, and a variety of cured meats, and Turkish cuisine features kebabs, baklava, and a wide array of mezze dishes.

The concept of communal dining is integral to Mediterranean culture, with meals often seen as a time for family and friends to come together. Shared platters of mezze, or small appetizers, are a common feature, encouraging a social and relaxed dining experience. This emphasis on community and the enjoyment of food as a shared experience adds a unique dimension to Mediterranean cuisine.

In terms of cooking techniques, the Mediterranean region employs methods that highlight the natural flavors of ingredients. Grilling, roasting, and slow cooking are prevalent, allowing for the development of rich, nuanced tastes. The use of fresh, local produce is paramount, ensuring that dishes are not only delicious but also reflect the seasonality of ingredients.

Now, turning our attention to the Mediterranean Crock Pot, this cooking appliance aligns well with the principles of Mediterranean cuisine. The slow-cooking method allows for the melding of flavors and the tenderization of meats, creating dishes that are both convenient and full of depth. It's an ideal tool for

recreating traditional Mediterranean recipes that often involve simmering stews, braising meats, and infusing dishes with aromatic herbs and spices.

In the Mediterranean Crock Pot recipe book, you can explore a wide range of dishes inspired by the diverse culinary traditions of the Mediterranean. From hearty Italian minestrone soup to Greek lamb stew with olives and rosemary, and Moroccan chickpea tagine with aromatic spices, the possibilities are extensive. These recipes not only celebrate the vibrant flavors of the Mediterranean but also provide a convenient and modern twist to traditional dishes.

In conclusion, Mediterranean cuisine is a rich tapestry of flavors, ingredients, and cultural influences that has captivated food enthusiasts around the world. By embracing the principles of a balanced and healthy diet, the use of fresh and seasonal ingredients, and the communal spirit of shared meals, the Mediterranean Crock Pot recipe book can offer a delightful culinary journey for anyone looking to savor the essence of this captivating culinary tradition.

Mediterranean Flavors

Mediterranean cuisine is a rich tapestry of flavors, colors, and textures that

reflect the diverse cultures surrounding the Mediterranean Sea. When it comes to creating a delightful Mediterranean Crock Pot dish, the emphasis is on fresh and wholesome ingredients, often inspired by the sun-kissed landscapes of Greece, Italy, Spain, and other coastal regions.

One of the defining characteristics of Mediterranean flavors is the use of olive oil as a primary cooking fat. Olive oil not only adds a distinct taste but also brings health benefits, being a key component of the Mediterranean diet. Its fruity and robust notes complement a variety of dishes, enhancing the overall culinary experience. When preparing a Mediterranean Crock Pot recipe, be generous with the extra virgin olive oil to infuse your dish with that characteristic Mediterranean essence.

Herbs play a pivotal role in Mediterranean cuisine, offering a burst of freshness and aromatic complexity. Basil, oregano, thyme, rosemary, and parsley are staples in the Mediterranean flavor palette. Incorporate these herbs liberally into your Crock Pot recipes to elevate the taste profile. Whether you're slow-cooking a tomato-based stew or marinating meat, the herbs will infuse a fragrant bouquet that transports you to the sun-drenched hillsides of southern Europe.

Citrus fruits, particularly lemons, add a zesty brightness to Mediterranean dishes. The tangy acidity of lemon juice can balance the richness of olive oil and bring a refreshing note to savory stews, grilled meats, or seafood. When crafting your Crock Pot masterpiece, squeeze fresh lemon juice into your recipe or add lemon slices to infuse a subtle citrus undertone that enhances the overall complexity of flavors.

Mediterranean cuisine also embraces a vibrant array of vegetables, showcasing

the region's bountiful harvest. Tomatoes, eggplants, bell peppers, zucchini, and artichokes are commonly used in various dishes. When preparing a Mediterranean Crock Pot recipe, include a colorful assortment of these vegetables to create a visually appealing and nutritionally rich dish. Slow cooking allows the vegetables to meld together, intensifying their flavors and creating a harmonious blend.

Proteins such as fish, poultry, lamb, and legumes are integral components of Mediterranean meals. Fish, in particular, is often grilled or baked to perfection. For a Crock Pot dish, consider using boneless, skinless chicken thighs or lean cuts of lamb. The slow-cooking process allows the proteins to absorb the surrounding flavors, resulting in tender and succulent bites that encapsulate the essence of Mediterranean cuisine.

Mediterranean Crock Pot recipes often include olives and capers, which contribute a briny and salty kick. Kalamata and green olives, along with capers, bring a unique dimension to your dish, adding depth and complexity. Incorporate them strategically into your slow-cooked creation to impart that unmistakable Mediterranean tang.

Finally, don't forget about garlic. Garlic is a fundamental ingredient in Mediterranean cooking, imparting a robust and savory taste. Whether minced, sliced, or roasted, garlic enhances the overall flavor profile of your Crock Pot dish, creating a satisfying and aromatic experience.

In conclusion, crafting a Mediterranean Crock Pot dish involves a thoughtful combination of extra virgin olive oil, aromatic herbs, citrusy notes, vibrant vegetables, high-quality proteins, olives, capers, and the indispensable touch of garlic. By embracing these key elements, you can create a slow-cooked masterpiece that captures the essence of the Mediterranean and delights the senses with every savory bite.

Crock Pot Basics for Mediterranean Cooking

The slow cooker, commonly known as a Crock Pot, is an indispensable tool in the kitchen, especially when preparing Mediterranean dishes. Its ability to simmer and stew ingredients over an extended period not only enhances flavors but also makes meal preparation more convenient. Let's delve into the essential Crock

Pot basics for mastering the art of Mediterranean cooking.

- Choosing the Right Crock Pot:

  Selecting the appropriate size for your Crock Pot is crucial. For Mediterranean recipes, a 6 to 7-quart slow cooker is generally ideal. This size allows for accommodating a variety of ingredients and is perfect for preparing family-sized meals.

- Understanding Temperature Settings:

  Most Crock Pots come with three temperature settings: Low, High, and Warm. Low is perfect for slow-cooking, allowing flavors to meld gradually. High is for quicker cooking and is useful when time is limited. Warm is for keeping food at a safe serving temperature once the cooking process is complete.

- Prepping Ingredients:

  Mediterranean cuisine is known for its fresh and wholesome ingredients. Chop vegetables, trim meats, and prepare other components before placing them in the Crock Pot. This not only saves time but also ensures even cooking.

- Layering Ingredients:

  Layering ingredients strategically is essential in a Crock Pot to promote even cooking. Place root vegetables at the bottom, followed by protein and grains, and top it off with herbs and spices. This arrangement helps ingredients cook uniformly, resulting in a harmonious blend of flavors.

- Liquids and Broths:

  Mediterranean dishes often rely on robust flavors, and using the right liquids is crucial. Utilize chicken or vegetable broth, wine, or citrus juices to infuse richness into your recipes. These liquids not only enhance taste but also keep the dish moist during the slow-cooking process.

- Herbs and Spices:

  Mediterranean cuisine is renowned for its aromatic herbs and spices. Incorporate staples like oregano, thyme, rosemary, garlic, and olive oil for an authentic taste. Add these towards the end of the cooking time to preserve their freshness and intensity.

- Timing is Key:

  One of the Crock Pot's virtues is its ability to transform tough cuts of meat into tender masterpieces. Ensure you follow the recommended cooking times in your recipes to achieve the desired texture and flavors. Overcooking can lead to mushy vegetables or dried-out meats.

- Adapting Recipes for the Crock Pot:

  Not all recipes are inherently suited for slow cooking. Modify traditional

Mediterranean recipes by adjusting liquid content and selecting ingredients that withstand prolonged cooking times. Experimentation is key to finding the perfect balance for your Crock Pot creations.

- Avoiding Dairy Early:

  Dairy products like feta or yogurt are common in Mediterranean cuisine, but they're best added towards the end of the cooking process. Adding them too early can result in separation or curdling. Stirring in these ingredients just before serving maintains their creamy consistency.

- Finishing Touches:

  The final steps are crucial for achieving a Mediterranean masterpiece. Adjust seasoning, add fresh herbs, and a drizzle of extra virgin olive oil before serving to elevate the dish's flavors.

In conclusion, mastering Mediterranean Crock Pot cooking involves understanding the nuances of this versatile kitchen appliance. By incorporating these Crock Pot basics into your culinary routine, you'll be on your way to creating delectable, flavorful, and authentic Mediterranean dishes that are sure to impress your taste buds and those of your loved ones.

Tips and Tricks to Make Mediterranean Cooking Easier

Mediterranean cooking is renowned for its vibrant flavors, fresh ingredients, and health benefits. To make the most of your culinary journey with a Mediterranean Crock Pot, here are some tips and tricks that will simplify the process and enhance your cooking experience.

- Embrace Fresh and Seasonal Ingredients:

  One of the key elements of Mediterranean cuisine is the use of fresh, seasonal produce. Incorporate a variety of colorful vegetables, ripe tomatoes, leafy greens, and aromatic herbs into your recipes. Visit local markets or grocery stores to ensure you're using the best-quality ingredients available.

- Invest in Quality Olive Oil:

  Olive oil is a staple in Mediterranean cooking, adding richness and depth to dishes. Choose extra virgin olive oil for its robust flavor and health benefits. Drizzle it over salads, use it as a base for marinades, or finish off your dishes with a splash for an authentic touch.

- Master the Art of Herbs and Spices:

  Herbs and spices play a crucial role in Mediterranean cuisine, offering a burst of flavor without excessive use of salt or fat. Familiarize yourself with classics like oregano, thyme, rosemary, and basil. Experiment with spices such as cumin, coriander, and paprika to elevate your dishes.

- Plan Ahead with Batch Cooking:

  Simplify your meal preparation by embracing batch cooking. Prepare larger quantities of key components like grains, legumes, or roasted vegetables and store them for later use. This will save time on busy days and allow you to assemble delicious meals with minimal effort.

- Optimize Your Crock Pot:

  The slow cooker, or Crock Pot, can be a game-changer in Mediterranean cooking. It allows flavors to meld and intensify over time, resulting in rich and satisfying dishes. Experiment with recipes like slow-cooked stews, soups, or braised meats that capture the essence of Mediterranean cuisine.

- Choose Lean Proteins:

  Mediterranean diets often emphasize lean protein sources such as fish, poultry, and legumes. Incorporate these into your Crock Pot recipes for a healthy and balanced approach. Fish stews, chickpea-based dishes, or slow-cooked chicken with Mediterranean spices are excellent choices.

- Don't Forget Citrus:

  Citrus fruits, such as lemons and oranges, add a zesty and refreshing touch to many Mediterranean dishes. Use citrus juices and zest to brighten up your slow-cooked meals. It's a simple yet effective way to enhance flavors without relying on heavy sauces.

- Experiment with Mediterranean Grains:

  Expand your grain repertoire beyond the usual suspects. Integrate ancient grains like farro, quinoa, or bulgur into your recipes for added nutritional benefits and unique textures. These grains complement the Mediterranean flavor profile and contribute to a well-rounded meal.

- Incorporate Nuts and Seeds:

  To add crunch and nutritional value, include a variety of nuts and seeds in your Mediterranean Crock Pot creations. Pine nuts, almonds, and sesame seeds can be sprinkled over finished dishes for a delightful texture and extra layers of flavor.

- Celebrate Simple Meals:

  Mediterranean cuisine celebrates the beauty of simplicity. Embrace the

concept of a few high-quality ingredients coming together to create a satisfying meal. Allow the natural flavors to shine through, and don't be afraid to keep some recipes uncomplicated.

In conclusion, mastering the art of Mediterranean cooking with a Crock Pot involves a combination of quality ingredients, strategic planning, and a willingness to explore diverse flavors. By incorporating these tips and tricks into your culinary repertoire, you'll find joy in creating wholesome and delicious meals that reflect the essence of the Mediterranean lifestyle.

Why are Crock Pots Good for the Mediterranean Diet

The Mediterranean Diet is renowned for its emphasis on fresh, wholesome ingredients, heart-healthy fats, and a balanced approach to nutrition. When considering the virtues of the Crock Pot in the context of this diet, several factors come into play, making it a remarkably suitable cooking method that aligns well with the principles of Mediterranean cuisine.

Firstly, the Mediterranean Diet places great importance on the consumption of vegetables, legumes, and lean proteins, all of which can be easily incorporated into Crock Pot recipes. The slow-cooking process allows these ingredients to meld together, enhancing their flavors and preserving their nutritional value. Vegetables like tomatoes, bell peppers, zucchini, and eggplant, often staples in Mediterranean cooking, benefit from the slow simmering of a Crock Pot, developing rich, savory profiles that contribute to the overall taste of a dish.

Moreover, the use of olive oil, a cornerstone of the Mediterranean Diet, pairs seamlessly with the Crock Pot's low and slow cooking method. The gentle heat helps infuse the dishes with the distinct fruity and peppery notes of extra virgin olive oil, enhancing the authenticity of Mediterranean flavors. This cooking technique also promotes the breakdown of tougher cuts of meat, turning them tender and succulent, aligning with the diet's preference for lean protein sources like fish and poultry.

In addition to enhancing flavor, the Crock Pot supports the Mediterranean Diet's commitment to convenience and simplicity. The one-pot nature of many Crock Pot recipes streamlines the cooking process, reducing the need for multiple pots and pans. This not only makes meal preparation more straightforward but also minimizes cleanup, encouraging adherence to the diet by making it more accessible to those with busy lifestyles.

The Crock Pot's gentle and consistent heat is particularly advantageous for Mediterranean dishes that often involve slow-cooking methods. Traditional Mediterranean recipes such as stews, soups, and braised dishes benefit from the Crock Pot's ability to maintain a low, even temperature over an extended period, allowing the flavors to meld harmoniously. This slow infusion of flavors is emblematic of the Mediterranean approach to savoring meals, promoting a more relaxed and enjoyable dining experience.

Furthermore, the Crock Pot's versatility complements the diverse range of ingredients found in the Mediterranean Diet. Whether it's grains, legumes, or an array of vegetables, the Crock Pot accommodates various elements, enabling the creation of hearty and satisfying meals that embody the essence of Mediterranean cuisine. The adaptability of the Crock Pot encourages culinary experimentation, making it easy for individuals to personalize their dishes while still adhering to the principles of the Mediterranean Diet.

In conclusion, the Crock Pot's slow-cooking method aligns seamlessly with the Mediterranean Diet's emphasis on fresh, wholesome ingredients, heart-healthy fats, and a balanced approach to nutrition. Its ability to enhance flavors, simplify meal preparation, and accommodate a wide range of ingredients makes it an excellent tool for those seeking to embrace the healthful and delicious aspects of Mediterranean cuisine in their own homes.

Chapter 1: Soups and Stews

Chicken & Chickpea Soup

Prep Time: 20 Minutes Cook Time: 4 Hours Serves: 6

Ingredients:

- 1 ½ cups dried chickpeas, soaked overnight
- 4 cups water
- 1 large yellow onion, finely chopped
- 1 (15 ounce) can no-salt-added diced tomatoes, preferably fire-roasted
- 2 tablespoons tomato paste
- 4 cloves garlic, finely chopped
- 1 bay leaf
- 4 teaspoons ground cumin
- 4 teaspoons paprika
- ¼ teaspoon cayenne pepper
- ¼ teaspoon ground pepper
- 2 pounds bone-in chicken thighs, skin removed, trimmed
- 1 (14 ounce) can artichoke hearts, drained and quartered
- ¼ cup halved pitted oil-cured olives
- ½ teaspoon salt
- ¼ cup chopped fresh parsley or cilantro

Directions:

1. Drain chickpeas and place in a large crock pot.
2. Add water, onion, tomatoes and their juice, tomato paste, garlic, bay leaf, cumin, paprika, cayenne and pepper; stir to combine.
3. Cover and cook on Low for 8 hours or High for 4 hours.
4. Transfer the chicken to a clean cutting board and let cool slightly. Discard bay leaf. Add artichokes, olives and salt to the crock pot and stir to combine.
5. Shred the chicken, discarding bones. Stir the chicken into the soup.
6. Serve topped with parsley (or cilantro).

Nutritional Value (Amount per Serving):

Calories: 631; Fat: 28.46; Carb: 40.24; Protein: 54.34

White Bean, Spinach & Sausage Stew

Prep Time: 30 Minutes Cook Time: 7 Hours 20 Minutes Serves: 6

Ingredients:

- 2 cups dried cannellini beans
- 5 cups unsalted chicken stock

- 1 plum tomato, stem end trimmed (about 5 ounces)
- 1 teaspoon kosher salt
- ½ teaspoon black pepper
- 4 garlic cloves, lightly crushed
- 2 fresh rosemary sprigs
- 6 ounces spinach-and-feta chicken-and-turkey sausage, cut diagonally into 1/2-inch-thick slices
- 5 ounces baby spinach, roughly chopped
- ¼ cup chopped fresh flat-leaf parsley
- 2 tablespoons extra-virgin olive oil

Directions:

1. Sort and wash the beans; place in a large Dutch oven. Cover with water to 2 inches above the beans; cover and let stand 8 hours.
2. Drain the beans. Place the beans in a crock pot. Add the stock, tomato, salt, pepper, garlic, and rosemary sprigs.
3. Cover and cook on LOW until the beans are tender, about 7 hours.
4. Lightly mash the bean mixture with a potato masher, breaking up the tomato and garlic. Add the sausage to the crock pot; cover and cook on LOW until thoroughly heated, about 20 minutes.
5. Add the spinach and parsley, stirring just until the spinach begins to wilt. Discard the rosemary sprigs.
6. Ladle the stew into bowls; drizzle evenly with the oil before serving.

Nutritional Value (Amount per Serving):

Calories: 987; Fat: 26.87; Carb: 6.12; Protein: 170.27

Mediterranean Diet Stew

Prep Time: 15 Minutes Cook Time: 6 Hours 30 Minutes Serves: 6

Ingredients:

- 2 (14 ounce) cans no-salt-added fire-roasted diced tomatoes
- 3 cups low-sodium vegetable broth
- 1 cup coarsely chopped onion
- ¾ cup chopped carrot
- 4 cloves garlic, minced
- 1 teaspoon dried oregano
- ¾ teaspoon salt
- ½ teaspoon crushed red pepper
- ¼ teaspoon ground pepper
- 1 (15 ounce) can no-salt-added chickpeas, rinsed, divided
- 1 bunch lacinato kale, stemmed and chopped (about 8 cups)

- 1 tablespoon lemon juice
- 3 tablespoons extra-virgin olive oil
- Fresh basil leaves, torn if large
- 6 lemon wedges (Optional)

Directions:

1. Combine tomatoes, broth, onion, carrot, garlic, oregano, salt, crushed red pepper and pepper in a crock pot. Cover and cook on Low for 6 hours.
2. Measure 1/4 cup of the cooking liquid from the crock pot into a small bowl. Add 2 tablespoons chickpeas; mash with a fork until smooth.
3. Add the mashed chickpeas, kale, lemon juice and remaining whole chickpeas to the mixture in the crock pot. Stir to combine. Cover and cook on Low until the kale is tender, about 30 minutes.
4. Ladle the stew evenly into 6 bowls; drizzle with oil. Garnish with basil. Serve with lemon wedges, if desired.

Nutritional Value (Amount per Serving):

Calories: 143; Fat: 4.79; Carb: 24.33; Protein: 6.7

Chicken & Vegetable Noodle Soup

Prep Time: 15 Minutes Cook Time: 3 Hours 35 Minutes Serves: 6

Ingredients:

- 1 pound boneless, skinless chicken breast
- 1 (14 ounce) can no-salt-added fire-roasted diced tomatoes
- 4 cups low-sodium chicken broth
- 1 ½ cups chopped yellow onion
- 1 cup chopped orange bell pepper
- 4 cloves garlic, minced
- 1 tablespoon Italian seasoning
- ½ teaspoon ground pepper
- ¼ teaspoon salt
- ¼ teaspoon crushed red pepper
- 1 bay leaf
- 6 ounces whole-wheat rotini pasta
- 2 tablespoons chopped fresh basil
- 2 tablespoons chopped fresh flat-leaf parsley, plus more for garnish
- ½ cup grated Parmesan cheese

Directions:

1. Combine chicken, tomatoes, broth, onion, bell pepper, garlic, Italian seasoning, pepper, salt, crushed red pepper and bay leaf in a crock pot.
2. Cover and cook on High until the chicken is tender and an instant-read

thermometer inserted into the thickest part of the chicken registers 165 degrees F, about 3 hours.
3. Remove and discard the bay leaf. Transfer the chicken to a plate; let rest for 10 minutes.
4. Meanwhile, stir pasta into the mixture in the slow cooker; cover and cook on High until the pasta is tender, about 30 minutes.
5. Coarsely shred the chicken and stir it back into the soup, along with basil and parsley. Ladle the soup evenly into 6 bowls; sprinkle with Parmesan and garnish with parsley, if desired.

Nutritional Value (Amount per Serving):

Calories: 293; Fat: 11.31; Carb: 33.48; Protein: 15.43

Lemon Chicken-and-Egg Soup

Prep Time: 30 Minutes Cook Time: 4 Hours 15 Minutes Serves: 8

Ingredients:

- 2 ½ pounds bone-in, skin-on chicken breasts
- 6 cups low-sodium chicken broth
- 3 cups frozen corn kernels
- 4 1/4-inch-thick coins fresh ginger
- 2 ½ tablespoons reduced-sodium tamari or soy sauce
- 2 large eggs
- 1 teaspoon cornstarch
- ½ teaspoon toasted sesame oil, plus more for serving
- ⅛ teaspoon salt
- 6 tablespoons lemon juice
- ¼ cup fresh cilantro leaves
- 1 tablespoon toasted sesame seeds

Directions:

1. Put chicken in a crock pot and add broth, corn, ginger and tamari (or soy sauce). Cover and cook until the chicken reaches an internal temperature of 165°F, about 4 hours on High or 6 hours on Low.
2. Set the crock pot to High, if it isn't already. Discard the ginger. Transfer the chicken to a bowl. Put the lid back on so the broth comes to a gentle simmer at the edges. Remove and discard the chicken skin and bones; shred the chicken.
3. Whisk eggs, cornstarch, sesame oil and salt in a glass measuring cup. Gradually drizzle the mixture into the very hot soup, stirring gently with a fork; the mixture will form fine strands as it cooks.
4. Return the chicken to the soup, cover and cook for 15 minutes. Stir in

lemon juice.

5. Top the soup with cilantro, sesame seeds and a few drops of sesame oil, if desired.

Nutritional Value (Amount per Serving):

Calories: 268; Fat: 6.43; Carb: 22.32; Protein: 31.53

Turkey & Kale Minestrone Soup

Prep Time: 20 Minutes Cook Time: 3 Hours 30 Minutes Serves: 10

Ingredients:

- 10 ounces spicy turkey Italian sausage, casings removed
- 2 cups chopped yellow onions (from 1 onion)
- 1 cup chopped carrots (from 1 carrot)
- ¾ cup chopped celery (from 2 celery stalks)
- 6 cups unsalted chicken stock
- 2 (14.5 ounce) cans no-salt-added fire-roasted diced tomatoes, undrained
- 1 (15 ounce) can no-salt-added kidney beans, drained and rinsed
- 1 teaspoon kosher salt
- ½ teaspoon black pepper
- 1 cup uncooked ditalini pasta
- 2 cups packed fresh baby kale leaves, roughly chopped

Directions:

1. Heat a large nonstick skillet over medium-high. Add the sausage to the skillet, and cook, stirring to crumble with a wooden spoon, 4 minutes.
2. Add the onions, carrots, and celery to the skillet; cook, stirring occasionally, until the sausage is browned and the vegetables are lightly caramelized, about 6 minutes.
3. Add 1 cup of the stock; cook 1 minute, stirring and scraping to loosen the browned bits from the bottom of the skillet.
4. Transfer the sausage mixture to a slow cooker. Stir in the tomatoes, beans, salt, 1/4 teaspoon of the pepper, and the remaining 5 cups stock.
5. Cover and cook on LOW until the vegetables are tender, about 2 hours and 30 minutes. Stir in the pasta; cover and cook on LOW until the pasta is al dente, about 1 hour.
6. Stir in the kale and remaining 1/4 teaspoon pepper. Ladle the soup into bowls, and serve hot.

Nutritional Value (Amount per Serving):

Calories: 735; Fat: 20.09; Carb: 9.59; Protein: 121.78

Lentil, Carrot & Potato Soup

Prep Time: 30 Minutes   Cook Time: 7 Hours   Serves: 8

Ingredients:

- 4 cups unsalted vegetable stock
- 4 cups water
- 2 cups chopped peeled sweet potato (from 1 sweet potato)
- 2 cups sliced carrots (from 3 carrots)
- 2 cups chopped peeled russet potato (from 1 potato)
- 1 ½ cups dried green lentils
- 1 ½ cups chopped yellow onions (from 1 onion)
- 1 cup chopped celery (from 2 celery stalks)
- 2 tablespoons minced garlic (from 6 garlic cloves)
- 4 fresh thyme sprigs
- 1 bay leaf
- 1 ⅛ teaspoons kosher salt
- 1 teaspoon black pepper
- 6 tablespoons olive oil
- 3 tablespoons apple cider vinegar
- ¼ cup chopped fresh flat-leaf parsley

Directions:

1. Stir together the stock, water, sweet potato, carrots, russet potato, lentils, onions, celery, garlic, thyme sprigs, bay leaf, salt, and pepper in a slow cooker.
2. Cover and cook on LOW until the vegetables and lentils are tender, 7 to 8 hours. Remove and discard the thyme sprigs and bay leaf.
3. Place the oil and 4 cups of the soup in a blender. Remove the center piece of the blender lid (to allow steam to escape); secure the blender lid on the blender. Place a clean towel over the opening in the lid (to avoid splatters).
4. Process until smooth. Return the pureed soup to the slow cooker; stir in the vinegar. Ladle the soup into bowls, and sprinkle evenly with the parsley.

Nutritional Value (Amount per Serving):

Calories: 230; Fat: 12.27; Carb: 26.34; Protein: 5.55

Slow-Cooker Vegetable Soup

Prep Time: 35 Minutes   Cook Time: 4 Hours   Serves: 8

Ingredients:

- 1 medium onion, chopped

- 2 medium carrots, chopped
- 2 stalks celery, chopped
- 12 ounces fresh green beans, cut into 1/2-inch pieces
- 4 cups chopped kale
- 2 medium zucchinis, chopped
- 4 Roma tomatoes, seeded and chopped
- 2 cloves garlic, minced
- 2 (15 ounce) cans no-salt-added cannellini or other white beans, rinsed
- 4 cups low-sodium chicken broth or low-sodium vegetable broth
- 1 Parmesan rind (optional)
- 2 teaspoons salt
- ½ teaspoon ground pepper
- 2 teaspoons red-wine vinegar
- 8 teaspoons prepared pesto

Directions:

1. Combine onion, carrots, celery, green beans, kale, zucchini, tomatoes, garlic, white beans, broth, Parmesan rind (if using), salt and pepper in a large slow cooker.
2. Cover and cook on High for 4 hours or on Low for 6 hours.
3. Remove Parmesan rind, if using.
4. Stir in vinegar and top each serving of soup with 1 teaspoon pesto.

Nutritional Value (Amount per Serving):

Calories: 98; Fat: 5.32; Carb: 10.36; Protein: 4.21

Slow-Cooker Vegetable Minestrone Soup

Prep Time: 30 Minutes Cook Time: 6 Hours Serves: 8

Ingredients:

- 4 large carrots, peeled and chopped
- 3 stalks celery, chopped
- 1 small red onion, chopped
- 3 cloves garlic, minced
- 2 cups fresh green beans, trimmed and cut into 2-inch pieces
- 2 (15 ounce) cans no-sodium-added red kidney beans, rinsed
- 2 (15 ounce) cans no-sodium-added diced tomatoes, undrained
- 6 cups no-sodium-added vegetable broth
- 2 tablespoons Italian seasoning
- 1 teaspoon crushed red pepper
- ¾ teaspoon salt, divided
- ½ teaspoon ground pepper

- 1 large zucchini, chopped
- 4 ounces whole-wheat pasta elbows or other small pasta (about 1 cup)
- ½ cup freshly grated Parmesan cheese

Directions:

1. Combine carrots, celery, onion, garlic, green beans, kidney beans, tomatoes, broth, Italian seasoning, crushed red pepper, 1/4 teaspoon salt, and pepper in a slow cooker.
2. Cover and cook on Low for 6 to 8 hours.
3. Stir in zucchini, pasta, and the remaining 1/2 teaspoon salt. Cover and cook on Low until the pasta are tender, 15 to 20 more minutes.
4. Serve immediately, topping each serving with about 1 1/2 tablespoons Parmesan.

Nutritional Value (Amount per Serving):

Calories: 328; Fat: 3.38; Carb: 36.83; Protein: 37.69

Moroccan-Spiced Chicken Stew

Prep Time: 30 Minutes Cook Time: 5 Hours Serves: 8

Ingredients:

- 1 teaspoon ground cumin
- ½ teaspoon ground cinnamon
- ½ teaspoon ground coriander
- ¼ teaspoon cayenne pepper
- 8 skinless, boneless chicken thighs (about 2 1/4 pounds), trimmed
- 2 tablespoons olive oil
- 1 cup vertically sliced yellow onions (from 1 onion)
- 2 teaspoons minced fresh ginger
- 1 ½ cups unsalted chicken stock
- 1 ½ cups chopped peeled sweet potato (from 1 sweet potato)
- 1 (28 ounce) can no-salt-added whole peeled tomatoes
- 1 (15 ounce) can no-salt-added chickpeas (garbanzo beans), drained and rinsed
- ¼ cup golden raisins
- 1 ½ teaspoons kosher salt
- 1 teaspoon lemon zest plus 1 1/2 tablespoons fresh juice (from 1 lemon)
- ¼ cup fresh cilantro sprigs (Optional)

Directions:

1. Stir together the cumin, cinnamon, coriander, and cayenne pepper in a small bowl. Sprinkle the chicken thighs evenly with the spice mixture. Heat 1 tablespoon of the oil in a large nonstick skillet over medium-high.

Add half of the chicken to the skillet; cook until browned on 1 side, about 5 minutes. Turn the chicken over, and cook 1 minute. Transfer the chicken to a slow cooker. Repeat the procedure with the remaining oil and chicken.

2. Add the onions and ginger to the skillet; cook, stirring often, until slightly softened, about 3 minutes. Add the stock to the skillet; cook 1 minute, stirring and scraping to loosen the browned bits from the bottom of the skillet. Transfer the onion mixture to the slow cooker. Stir the sweet potato into the slow cooker.
3. Using kitchen scissors, chop the tomatoes in the can. Stir the chopped tomatoes and tomato liquid, chickpeas, raisins, and salt into the slow cooker. Cover and cook on LOW until the chicken is done and the vegetables are tender, about 5 hours. Remove the chicken to a cutting board; cut or tear into bite-sized pieces. Stir the lemon zest and lemon juice into the mixture in the slow cooker; gently stir in the chicken. Ladle the stew into bowls, and top with the cilantro, if desired.

Nutritional Value (Amount per Serving):

Calories: 427; Fat: 12.08; Carb: 9.58; Protein: 67.07

Slow-Cooker Moroccan Lentil Soup

Prep Time: 30 Minutes Cook Time: 5 Hours Serves: 12

Ingredients:

- 2 cups chopped onions
- 2 cups chopped carrots
- 4 cloves garlic, minced
- 2 teaspoons extra-virgin olive oil
- 1 teaspoon ground cumin
- 1 teaspoon ground coriander
- 1 teaspoon ground turmeric
- ¼ teaspoon ground cinnamon
- ¼ teaspoon ground pepper
- 6 cups vegetable broth or reduced sodium chicken broth
- 2 cups water
- 3 cups chopped cauliflower
- 1 ¾ cups dried green lentils
- 1 (28 ounce) can diced tomatoes
- 2 tablespoons tomato paste
- 4 cups chopped fresh spinach or one (10 ounce) package frozen chopped spinach, thawed
- ½ cup chopped fresh cilantro
- 2 tablespoons lemon juice

Directions:

1. Combine onions, carrots, garlic, oil, cumin, coriander, turmeric, cinnamon and pepper in a slow cooker.
2. Add broth, water, cauliflower, lentils, tomatoes and tomato paste and stir until well combined.
3. Cover and cook until the lentils are tender, 4 to 5 hours on High or 8 to 10 hours on Low.
4. During the last 30 minutes of cooking, stir in spinach. Just before serving, stir in cilantro and lemon juice.

Nutritional Value (Amount per Serving):

Calories: 816; Fat: 64.81; Carb: 39.46; Protein: 34.92

Kale, Wild Rice & Chicken Stew

Prep Time: 30 Minutes Cook Time: 3 Hours Serves: 8

Ingredients:

- 2 pounds boneless, skinless chicken thighs, trimmed
- 1 ½ teaspoons dried thyme, divided
- 1 ½ teaspoons salt
- ¼ teaspoon ground pepper
- 6 cups low-sodium chicken broth
- 10 ounces sliced mushrooms
- 1 cup chopped carrot
- 1 cup chopped celery
- 1 cup chopped onion
- 1 cup wild rice
- ½ cup dry sherry
- 2 cloves garlic, chopped
- 6 cups chopped stemmed kale
- 1 cup sour cream, divided
- 1 tablespoon lemon juice

Directions:

1. Sprinkle chicken with 1 teaspoon thyme, salt and pepper.
2. Place in a large slow cooker and add broth, mushrooms, carrot, celery, onion, rice, sherry and garlic. Stir to combine.
3. Cover and cook on High for 3 hours or on Low for 6 hours.
4. Remove the chicken to a clean cutting board and shred. Stir the chicken back into the stew along with kale, 1/2 cup sour cream, lemon juice and the remaining 1/2 teaspoon thyme.
5. Serve topped with a dollop of the remaining sour cream.

Nutritional Value (Amount per Serving):

Calories: 379; Fat: 11.13; Carb: 52.2; Protein: 20.19

Slow-Cooker Chicken & White Bean Stew

Prep Time: 15 Minutes Cook Time: 7 Hours 20 Minutes Serves: 6

Ingredients:

- 1 pound dried cannellini beans, soaked overnight and drained
- 6 cups unsalted chicken broth
- 1 cup chopped yellow onion
- 1 cup sliced carrots
- 1 teaspoon finely chopped fresh rosemary
- 1 (4 ounce) Parmesan cheese rind plus 2/3 cup grated Parmesan, divided
- 2 bone-in chicken breasts (1 pound each)
- 4 cups chopped kale
- 1 tablespoon lemon juice
- ½ teaspoon kosher salt
- ½ teaspoon ground pepper
- 2 tablespoons extra-virgin olive oil
- ¼ cup flat-leaf parsley leaves

Directions:

1. Combine beans, broth, onion, carrots, rosemary and Parmesan rind in a slow cooker. Top with chicken.
2. Cover and cook on Low until the beans and vegetables are tender, 7 to 8 hours.
3. Transfer the chicken to a clean cutting board; let stand until cool enough to handle, about 10 minutes. Shred the chicken, discarding bones.
4. Return the chicken to the slow cooker and stir in kale. Cover and cook on High until the kale is tender, 20 to 30 minutes.
5. Stir in lemon juice, salt and pepper; discard the Parmesan rind.
6. Serve the stew drizzled with oil and sprinkled with Parmesan and parsley.

Nutritional Value (Amount per Serving):

Calories: 365; Fat: 12.36; Carb: 25.95; Protein: 38.7

Slow-Cooker Pasta e Fagioli Soup Freezer Pack

Prep Time: 15 Minutes Cook Time: 8 Hours Serves: 6

Ingredients:

- 2 cups chopped onions

- 1 cup chopped carrots
- 1 cup chopped celery
- 1 pound cooked Meal-Prep Sheet-Pan Chicken Thighs, diced
- 4 cups cooked whole-wheat rotini pasta
- 6 cups reduced-sodium chicken broth
- 4 teaspoons dried Italian seasoning
- ¼ teaspoon salt
- 1 (15 ounce) can no-salt-added white beans, rinsed
- 4 cups baby spinach (half of a 5-ounce box)
- 4 tablespoons chopped fresh basil, divided (Optional)
- 2 tablespoons best-quality extra-virgin olive oil
- ½ cup grated Parmigiano-Reggiano cheese

Directions:

1. Place onions, carrots and celery in a large sealable plastic bag. Place cooled cooked chicken and cooked pasta together in another bag.
2. Seal both bags and freeze for up to 5 days. Defrost the bags in the refrigerator overnight before proceeding.
3. Transfer the vegetable mixture to a large slow cooker. Add broth, Italian seasoning and salt. Cover and cook on Low for 7 1/4 hours.
4. Add beans, spinach, 2 tablespoons basil, if using, and the defrosted chicken and pasta. Cook for 45 more minutes. Ladle the soup into bowls.
5. Drizzle a little oil into each bowl and top with cheese and the remaining 2 tablespoons basil, if desired.

Nutritional Value (Amount per Serving):

Calories: 597; Fat: 30.22; Carb: 52.07; Protein: 33.04

Chapter 2: Vegetables

Slow Cooker Ratatouille

Prep Time: 10 Minutes   Cook Time: 6 Hours   Serves: 6

Ingredients:

- 2 tbsp olive oil
- 1 red onion, sliced
- 2 garlic cloves
- 2 large aubergines, cut into 1.5cm pieces
- 3 courgettes, halved and cut into 2cm pieces
- 3 mixed peppers, cut into 2cm pieces
- 1 tbsp tomato purée
- 6 large ripe tomatoes, roughly chopped
- small bunch of basil, roughly chopped, plus a few extra leaves to serve
- few thyme sprigs
- 400g can plum tomatoes
- 1 tbsp red wine vinegar
- 1 tsp brown sugar
- sourdough, to serve (optional)

Directions:

1. Heat the oil in a large frying pan and fry the onion for 8 minutes until translucent.
2. Add the garlic and fry for 1 minute. Turn the heat to medium-high, add the aubergines and fry for 5 minutes until golden. Stir in the courgettes and peppers and fry for 5 more minutes until slightly soft.
3. Add the tomato purée, fresh tomatoes, herbs, canned tomatoes, vinegar, sugar and 1 tsp salt and bring to a boil.
4. Transfer to the crock pot and cook on low for 5-6 hours or until everything is soft and the sauce has thickened.
5. Season, scatter over some extra basil, and serve with sourdough, if you like.

Nutritional Value (Amount per Serving):

Calories: 460; Fat: 22.8; Carb: 32.49; Protein: 35.22

Slow Cooker Vegetable Lasagna

Prep Time: 30 Minutes   Cook Time: 2 Hours 30 Minutes   Serves: 4

Ingredients:

- 1 tbsp rapeseed oil
- 2 onions, sliced
- 2 large garlic cloves, chopped

- 2 large courgettes, diced (400g)
- 1 red and 1 yellow pepper, deseeded and roughly sliced
- 400g can chopped tomatoes
- 2 tbsp tomato purée
- 2 tsp vegetable bouillon
- 15g fresh basil, chopped plus a few leaves
- 1 large aubergine, sliced across length or width for maximum surface area
- 6 wholewheat lasagne sheets (105g)
- 125g vegetarian buffalo mozzarella, chopped

Directions:

1. Heat 1 tbsp rapeseed oil in a large non-stick pan and fry 2 sliced onions and 2 chopped large garlic cloves for 5 minutes, stirring frequently until softened.
2. Tip in 2 diced large courgettes, 1 red and 1 yellow pepper, both roughly sliced, and 400g chopped tomatoes with 2 tbsp tomato purée, 2 tsp vegetable bouillon and 15g chopped basil.
3. Stir well, cover and cook for 5 minutes. Don't be tempted to add more liquid as plenty of moisture will come from the vegetables once they start cooking.
4. Slice 1 large aubergine. Lay half the slices of aubergine in the base of the slow cooker and top with 3 sheets of lasagna.
5. Add a third of the ratatouille mixture, then the remaining aubergine slices, 3 more lasagna sheets, then the remaining ratatouille mixture.
6. Cover and cook on High for 2½ - 3 hours until the pasta and vegetables are tender. Turn off the machine.
7. Scatter 125g vegetarian buffalo mozzarella over the vegetables then cover and leave for 10 minutes to settle and melt the cheese.
8. Scatter with extra basil and serve with a handful of rocket.

Nutritional Value (Amount per Serving):

Calories: 250; Fat: 14.98; Carb: 19.4; Protein: 12

Sweet & Sour Slow-Cooker Red Cabbage

Prep Time: 5 Minutes Cook Time: 4 Hours Serves: 6

Ingredients:

- 1 red cabbage (about 1kg), quartered and finely shredded
- ½ tsp ground mixed spice
- 50g light brown soft sugar
- 75ml red wine vinegar
- large knob of butter

Directions:

1. Heat the slow cooker to low.
2. Tip in the cabbage, then scatter in the mixed spice, sugar and some salt and pepper. Pour in the vinegar, stir well, then dot over the butter. Put the lid on and cook for 3 hours 30 minutes until starting to soften
3. Remove the lid and cook for another 30 minutes until the cabbage is very tender and sticky, and the liquid has reduced. Taste for seasoning and serve. Once cool, will keep covered and chilled for up to three days, or frozen for up to two months.
4. Reheat in the slow cooker or a pan over a medium heat until piping hot.

Nutritional Value (Amount per Serving):

Calories: 90; Fat: 5.79; Carb: 9.04; Protein: 0.24

Slow Cooker Cheesy Creamed Greens

Prep Time: 10 Minutes Cook Time: 3 Hours 10 Minutes Serves: 6-8

Ingredients

- 50g butter
- ½ tbsp olive oil
- 1 onion, thinly sliced
- 400g cavolo nero
- 3 leeks, sliced
- 100ml stock
- 400ml double cream
- 1 heaped tsp Dijon mustard
- generous grating of nutmeg
- 40g grated Parmesan or vegetarian alternative

Directions:

1. Heat the slow cooker to low. Heat the butter and oil in a frying pan. Add the onion and fry for 5 minutes over a low heat until softened and translucent.
2. Add the cavolo nero to the pan and fry for 5 minutes or until beginning to wilt.
3. Tip into the slow cooker along with the leeks, stock and 300ml of the cream. Cook with the lid on for 3 hours, stirring occasionally.
4. Stir through the remaining cream, the mustard, nutmeg and cheese, as well as some seasoning just before serving. Will keep, covered, in the fridge for up to three days.
5. Reheat in the slow cooker on medium for 45 minutes-1 hour.

Nutritional Value (Amount per Serving):

Calories: 393; Fat: 34.01; Carb: 17.73; Protein: 6.83

Slow Cooker Spiced Root & Lentil Casserole

Prep Time: 20 Minutes Cook Time: 5 Hours 30 Minutes Serves: 4

Ingredients:

- 2 tbsp olive oil
- 1 onion, finely chopped
- 3 carrots, peeled and cut into 3cm slices
- 500g (about 5 medium) parsnips, peeled and cut into 3cm slices
- 3 garlic cloves, crushed
- 2 tbsp mild curry powder
- 1 tbsp smoked paprika
- 150g red lentils, rinsed
- 600ml hot vegan vegetable stock
- 2 bay leaves
- lemon juice, to serve

Directions:

1. Heat the slow cooker to low. Heat the oil in a frying pan and cook the onion for 10 minutes until soft and transparent. Add the carrots and parsnips and fry for 8-10 more minutes until the veg is just golden.
2. Stir in the garlic and spices, and fry for 4-5 minutes until fragrant, stirring. Add a splash of water if needed. Tip into the slow cooker and stir through the lentils, stock, bay and seasoning.
3. Close the lid and cook on low for 5-6 hours until the vegetables are tender and the sauce has thickened.
4. Check the seasoning and stir in the lemon juice to taste.
5. Serve with bread, rice, or potatoes, if you like.

Nutritional Value (Amount per Serving):

Calories: 1726; Fat: 172.2; Carb: 52.18; Protein: 11.84

Greek-Style Stuffed Peppers

Prep Time: 30 Minutes Cook Time: 4 Hours 30 Minutes Serves: 8

Ingredients:

- 2 tablespoons olive oil
- 1 small fennel bulb, chopped
- 1 small red onion, chopped
- 1 package (10 ounces) frozen chopped spinach, thawed and squeezed dry
- 3 garlic cloves, minced
- 2 each medium sweet yellow, orange, red and green peppers

- 1 can (28 ounces) crushed tomatoes, divided
- 1 pound ground lamb
- 1 cup cooked barley
- 1 cup crumbled feta cheese, plus more for serving
- 1/2 cup Greek olives, chopped
- 1-1/2 teaspoons dried oregano
- 1/2 teaspoon salt
- 1/2 teaspoon crushed red pepper flakes
- 1/2 teaspoon pepper
- Chopped fresh parsley, optional

Directions:

1. In a large skillet, heat oil over medium-high heat. Add fennel and onion; cook and stir until tender, 6-8 minutes. Add spinach and garlic; cook 1 minute longer. Cool slightly.
2. Cut and reserve tops from peppers; remove and discard seeds. Pour 1 cup crushed tomatoes into bottom of a slow cooker.
3. In a large bowl, combine lamb, barley, 1 cup cheese, olives and seasonings; add fennel mixture.
4. Spoon mixture into peppers; place in slow cooker. Pour remaining crushed tomatoes over peppers; replace pepper tops. Cook, covered, on low 4-1/2 to 5-1/2 hours, until peppers are tender.
5. Serve with additional feta and, if desired, chopped parsley.

Nutritional Value (Amount per Serving):

Calories: 267; Fat: 15.9; Carb: 16.12; Protein: 17.53

Oregano Green Beans with Toasted Pine Nuts

Prep Time: 15 Minutes Cook Time: 5 Hours Serves: 8

Ingredients:

- 2 pounds fresh thin french-style green beans, cut into 2-inch pieces
- 1/2 cup water
- 2 tablespoons minced fresh oregano
- 1/2 teaspoon onion powder
- 1/2 teaspoon salt
- 1/4 teaspoon celery salt
- 1/4 teaspoon pepper
- 1/2 cup pine nuts or sliced almonds, toasted

Directions:

1. In a slow cooker, combine all ingredients except pine nuts.
2. Cook, covered, on low until beans are tender, 5-6 hours.

3. Remove with a slotted spoon. Top with pine nuts.

Nutritional Value (Amount per Serving):

Calories: 120; Fat: 6.32; Carb: 14.84; Protein: 3.47

Spice Trade Beans & Bulgur

Prep Time: 30 Minutes Cook Time: 3 Hours 20 Minutes Serves: 10

Ingredients:

- 3 tablespoons canola oil, divided
- 2 medium onions, chopped
- 1 medium sweet red pepper, chopped
- 5 garlic cloves, minced
- 1 tablespoon ground cumin
- 1 tablespoon paprika
- 2 teaspoons ground ginger
- 1 teaspoon pepper
- 1/2 teaspoon ground cinnamon
- 1/2 teaspoon cayenne pepper
- 1-1/2 cups bulgur
- 1 can (28 ounces) crushed tomatoes
- 1 can (14-1/2 ounces) diced tomatoes, undrained
- 1 carton (32 ounces) vegetable broth
- 2 tablespoons brown sugar
- 2 tablespoons soy sauce
- 1 can (15 ounces) garbanzo beans or chickpeas, rinsed and drained
- 1/2 cup golden raisins
- Minced fresh cilantro, optional

Directions:

1. In a large skillet, heat 2 tablespoons oil over medium-high heat. Add onions and pepper; cook and stir until tender, 3-4 minutes. Add garlic and seasonings; cook 1 minute longer. Transfer to a slow cooker.
2. In same skillet, heat remaining oil over medium-high heat. Add bulgur; cook and stir until lightly browned, 2-3 minutes.
3. Add bulgur, tomatoes, broth, brown sugar and soy sauce to slow cooker. Cook, covered, on low 3-4 hours or until bulgur is tender.
4. Stir in beans and raisins; cook 30 minutes longer. If desired, sprinkle with cilantro.

Nutritional Value (Amount per Serving):

Calories: 951; Fat: 96.69; Carb: 27.54; Protein: 3.82

Slow-Cooked Potatoes with Spring Onions

Prep Time: 5 Minutes   Cook Time: 6 Hours   Serves: 12

Ingredients

- 4 pounds small red potatoes
- 8 green onions, chopped (about 1 cup)
- 1 cup chopped sweet onion
- 1/4 cup olive oil
- 1/2 teaspoon salt
- 1/2 teaspoon pepper

Directions:

1. In a slow cooker, combine all ingredients.
2. Cook, covered, on low until potatoes are tender, 6-8 hours.

Nutritional Value (Amount per Serving):

Calories: 168; Fat: 4.96; Carb: 29.02; Protein: 3.57

Slow-Cooker Marinated Mushrooms

Prep Time: 15 Minutes   Cook Time: 6 Hours   Serves: 5

Ingredients:

- 2 pounds medium fresh mushrooms
- 1 package (14.4 ounces) frozen pearl onions, thawed
- 4 garlic cloves, minced
- 2 cups reduced-sodium beef broth
- 1/2 cup dry red wine
- 3 tablespoons balsamic vinegar
- 3 tablespoons olive oil
- 1 teaspoon salt
- 1 teaspoon dried basil
- 1/2 teaspoon dried thyme
- 1/2 teaspoon pepper
- 1/4 teaspoon crushed red pepper flakes

Directions:

1. Place mushrooms, onions and garlic in a slow cooker.
2. In a small bowl, whisk remaining ingredients; pour over mushrooms.
3. Cook, covered, on low 6-8 hours or until mushrooms are tender.

Nutritional Value (Amount per Serving):

Calories: 303; Fat: 24.43; Carb: 10.44; Protein: 12.47

Slow Cooker Balsamic Brussels Sprouts

Prep Time: 10 Minutes Cook Time: 4 Hours Serves: 6

Ingredients:

- 2 pounds brussels sprouts, rinsed and halved
- 2 tablespoons olive oil
- salt and pepper
- toasted pinenuts for serving, if desired
- Parmesan cheese for serving, if desired
- ½ cup balsamic vinegar
- 1-2 tablespoons light brown sugar

Directions:

1. Add brussels sprouts and olive oil to a slow cooker. Sprinkle with salt and pepper to taste.
2. Cover and cook on low for 3-4 hours or on high for 1-2 hours or until tender.
3. While the brussels sprouts is cooking, make the balsamic reduction. (I make it about 30 minutes before the brussels sprouts are done)
4. Add balsamic vinegar and brown sugar to a small saucepan. Simmer for 10 minutes or until the sauce has reduced by half. Keep warm until ready to use.
5. When the brussels sprouts is ready, drizzle with the balsamic reduction and serve immediately with pine nuts and Parmesan cheese, if desired.

Nutritional Value (Amount per Serving):

Calories: 147; Fat: 6.09; Carb: 19.82; Protein: 6.12

Velveeta Broccoli Rice Casserole

Prep Time: 15 Minutes Cook Time: 4 Hours Serves: 6

Ingredients:

- 1½ cup minute rice
- ¾ lb. Velveeta cheese, cut into ½ inch cubes
- 14.4 ounces frozen broccoli chopped
- 1 teaspoon onion flakes or ¼ cup onion minced
- 1 can water chestnuts drained and diced, 8 oz.
- 10.5 ounces Cream of Mushroom Soup, use canned or click for homemade recipe
- 1 can unsalted chicken broth or beef broth, 10½ oz.
- 1 cup milk

- ¼ cup white wine optional
- ½ teaspoon black pepper ground
- 1 cup crushed Ritz crackers
- ¼ cup butter melted

Directions:

1. Spray slow cooker with nonstick cooking spray.
2. Combine all ingredients in slow cooker and stir thoroughly.
3. Cover and cook on HIGH 2 hours or on LOW 4 hours.
4. If desired, combine crushed crackers and melted butter. Sprinkle the cracker/butter mixture over cooked casserole and place under oven broiler to brown. It can burn quickly, so watch closely.
5. Enjoy!

Nutritional Value (Amount per Serving):

Calories: 389; Fat: 22.81; Carb: 37.59; Protein: 19.87

Garlic Parmesan Spaghetti Squash

Prep Time: 10 Minutes Cook Time: 4 Hours Serves: 8-10

Ingredients:

- 1 small (1-2 pound) spaghetti squash
- 6 tablespoons unsalted butter
- 3 cloves garlic, minced
- 1/4 cup heavy cream
- 1/3 cup freshly grated Parmesan
- chopped fresh parsley leaves for garnish
- salt and pepper to taste

Directions:

1. Carefully pierce your spaghetti squash with a sharp knife 6-8 times all around.
2. Place it in the bowl of your slow cooker and cook for 3-4 hours on high or 6-8 hours on low.
3. Once the squash is tender, remove from the slow cooker and allow to cool slightly.
4. Once you can safely handle it, slice lengthwise and scoop out seeds.
5. Using a fork, scrape the flesh to create long strands.
6. Return the flesh to the slow cooker and turn it on low. Add cream, garlic, and butter and stir to combine. Continue to cook on low, stirring occasionally, until thickened and creamy.
7. Add Parmesan and stir to combine. Taste and season with salt and pepper appropriately.

8. Serve immediately topped with additional Parmesan and chopped parsley.

Nutritional Value (Amount per Serving):

Calories: 98; Fat: 7.02; Carb: 7.72; Protein: 2.4

Mediterranean Ratatouille Quinoa

Prep Time: 20 Minutes Cook Time: 4 Hours Serves: 6

Ingredients:

- 1 cup of quinoa, rinsed and drained
- 2 cups of vegetable broth
- 1 eggplant, diced
- 2 zucchinis, diced
- 1 bell pepper, diced
- 1 red onion, diced
- 4 cloves of garlic, minced
- 2 (14-ounce) cans of diced tomatoes
- 2 tablespoons of olive oil
- 1 teaspoon of dried thyme
- 1 teaspoon of dried rosemary
- Salt and black pepper to taste
- Fresh basil leaves for garnish (optional)

Directions:

1. In the crock pot, combine the rinsed quinoa, vegetable broth, diced eggplant, diced zucchinis, diced bell pepper, diced red onion, minced garlic, diced tomatoes, olive oil, dried thyme, dried rosemary, salt, and black pepper.
2. Stir well to mix.
3. Cover and cook on low for 4 hours or until the quinoa is cooked.

Nutritional Value (Amount per Serving):

Calories: 198; Fat: 6.63; Carb: 30.71; Protein: 6.14

Creamed Spinach

Prep Time: 5 Minutes Cook Time: 2 Hours Serves: 4-6

Ingredients:

- 20 oz frozen chopped spinach (2-10 oz pkgs)
- ¼ cup butter, melted
- ½ cup sherry, can substitute chicken broth

- ½ cup cream cheese, softened
- 10.5 oz can cream of mushroom soup
- 1 oz package Italian dressing mix

Directions:

1. Thaw and squeeze out the liquid of your spinach.
2. Place your spinach in your crock pot.
3. Put your remaining ingredients in a mixer and mix on slow for two minutes.
4. Pour your cream cheese mixture over top of your spinach and gently mix with your spinach until well combined.
5. Cover and cook on low for 2-3 hours.

Nutritional Value (Amount per Serving):

Calories: 232; Fat: 20.18; Carb: 9.12; Protein: 6.7

Slow Cooker Pesto Quinoa Salad

Prep Time: 15 Minutes Cook Time: 2 Hours Serves: 4

Ingredients:

- 1 cup of quinoa, rinsed and drained
- 2 cups of vegetable broth
- 1 cup of cherry tomatoes, halved
- 1 cup of fresh mozzarella balls, halved
- 1/2 cup of basil pesto
- 1/4 cup of chopped fresh basil
- 2 cloves of garlic, minced
- Salt and black pepper to taste
- Grated Parmesan cheese for garnish (optional)

Directions:

1. In the crock pot, combine the rinsed quinoa, vegetable broth, cherry tomatoes, fresh mozzarella balls, basil pesto, chopped fresh basil, minced garlic, salt, and black pepper.
2. Stir well to mix.
3. Cover and cook on low for 2 hours or until the quinoa is cooked and the salad is flavorful and combined.
4. Garnish with grated Parmesan cheese before serving, if desired.

Nutritional Value (Amount per Serving):

Calories: 190; Fat: 2.81; Carb: 34.71; Protein: 7.35

Slow Cooker Coconut Curry Lentils

Prep Time: 30 Minutes Cook Time: 4 Hours Serves: 10

Ingredients:

- 1 yellow onion
- 2 cloves garlic
- 2 cups brown lentils
- 1 sweet potato (about 3/4 lb.)
- 2 carrots
- 3 Tbsp curry powder (hot or mild)
- 1/4 tsp ground cloves (optional)
- 1 15oz. can petite diced tomatoes
- 1 15oz. can tomato sauce
- 3 cups vegetable broth
- 1 14oz. can coconut milk (full fat)
- 10 cups cooked rice
- 1/2 red onion
- 1/2 bunch fresh cilantro or green onions

Directions:

1. Dice the onion and mince the garlic. Peel the sweet potato and carrots. Dice the sweet potato (1/4-1/2 inch cubes) and slice the carrots.
2. Add the onion, garlic, sweet potato, carrots, lentils, curry powder, cloves, diced tomatoes, tomato sauce, and vegetable broth to the slow cooker. Stir to combine. Place the lid on the slow cooker and cook on high for 4 hours or on low for 7-8 hours. Once cooked, the lentils should be tender and most of the liquid should be absorbed.
3. Stir the can of coconut milk into the lentils. Taste and adjust the salt or other spices as needed (the amount of salt needed will depend on the type of broth used and the salt content of the canned tomatoes).
4. To serve, add 1 cup cooked rice to a bowl followed by 1 cup of the lentil mixture. Top with finely diced red onion and fresh cilantro.

Nutritional Value (Amount per Serving):

Calories: 585; Fat: 36.18; Carb: 83.04; Protein: 21.27

Chapter 3: Poultry

Lemon Garlic Chicken

Prep Time: 15 Minutes   Cook Time: 4 Hours   Serves: 6-8

Ingredients:

- 2.5 lbs bone-in, skin-on chicken thighs
- 1 lemon, sliced
- 4 cloves garlic, minced
- 1 teaspoon dried oregano
- 1 teaspoon dried thyme
- Salt and pepper to taste
- 1/2 cup chicken broth
- 2 tablespoons olive oil

Directions:

1. Season chicken thighs with salt, pepper, oregano, and thyme.
2. Heat olive oil in a skillet over medium-high heat. Brown chicken on both sides.
3. Place chicken in the crock pot. Add lemon slices, minced garlic, and chicken broth.
4. Cover and cook on low for 4 hours or until chicken is tender.
5. Serve hot, garnished with fresh herbs if desired.

Nutritional Value (Amount per Serving):

Calories: 781; Fat: 76.74; Carb: 3.19; Protein: 19.51

Mediterranean Turkey Stew

Prep Time: 20 Minutes   Cook Time: 6 Hours   Serves: 6-8

Ingredients:

- 2 lbs turkey breast, cut into cubes
- 1 cup carrots, sliced
- 1 cup celery, diced
- 1 onion, chopped
- 3 cloves garlic, minced
- 1 cup cherry tomatoes, halved
- 1 cup green olives, pitted
- 2 teaspoons dried rosemary
- Salt and pepper to taste
- 2 cups chicken broth
- 1/4 cup tomato paste

Directions:

1. In the crock pot, combine turkey, carrots, celery, onion, garlic, tomatoes, and olives.
2. Mix rosemary, salt, pepper, chicken broth, and tomato paste in a bowl. Pour over the turkey and vegetables.
3. Cover and cook on low for 6 hours or until turkey is cooked through.
4. Serve over couscous or quinoa.

Nutritional Value (Amount per Serving):

Calories: 334; Fat: 14.02; Carb: 5.52; Protein: 44.11

Greek Yogurt Chicken

Prep Time: 15 Minutes Cook Time: 5 Hours Serves: 4-6

Ingredients:

- 2 lbs chicken breasts, boneless and skinless
- 1 cup Greek yogurt
- 3 tablespoons olive oil
- 4 cloves garlic, minced
- 1 teaspoon dried oregano
- 1 teaspoon dried thyme
- Salt and pepper to taste
- 1 lemon, juiced
- Fresh parsley for garnish

Directions:

1. In a bowl, mix Greek yogurt, olive oil, garlic, oregano, thyme, salt, pepper, and lemon juice.
2. Place chicken breasts in the crock pot and coat with the yogurt mixture.
3. Cook on low for 5 hours or until chicken is tender and cooked through.
4. Garnish with fresh parsley before serving.

Nutritional Value (Amount per Serving):

Calories: 401; Fat: 25; Carb: 2.96; Protein: 39.47

Mediterranean Chicken and Artichokes

Prep Time: 20 Minutes Cook Time: 4 Hours Serves: 6-8

Ingredients:

- 2.5 lbs chicken thighs, bone-in, skin-on
- 1 can (14 oz) artichoke hearts, drained and quartered
- 1 cup cherry tomatoes, halved
- 1 onion, thinly sliced
- 4 cloves garlic, minced
- 1 teaspoon dried basil
- 1 teaspoon dried oregano
- Salt and pepper to taste
- 1/2 cup chicken broth
- 2 tablespoons balsamic vinegar

Directions:

1. Season chicken thighs with basil, oregano, salt, and pepper.
2. Place chicken in the crock pot and add artichoke hearts, tomatoes, onion, and garlic.
3. Pour chicken broth and balsamic vinegar over the ingredients.
4. Cover and cook on low for 4 hours or until chicken is cooked through.
5. Serve over couscous or rice.

Nutritional Value (Amount per Serving):

Calories: 405; Fat: 28.19; Carb: 4.99; Protein: 31.28

Moroccan Spiced Chicken

Prep Time: 15 Minutes   Cook Time: 6 Hours   Serves: 6-8

Ingredients:

- 2.5 lbs chicken drumsticks
- 1 large sweet potato, peeled and diced
- 1 cup dried apricots
- 1 onion, chopped
- 3 cloves garlic, minced
- 1 teaspoon ground cumin
- 1 teaspoon ground coriander
- 1/2 teaspoon cinnamon
- Salt and pepper to taste
- 1 cup chicken broth
- Fresh cilantro for garnish

Directions:

1. In the crock pot, combine chicken drumsticks, sweet potato, apricots, onion, and garlic.
2. Mix cumin, coriander, cinnamon, salt, pepper, and chicken broth in a bowl. Pour over the chicken and vegetables.
3. Cover and cook on low for 6 hours or until chicken is tender.
4. Garnish with fresh cilantro before serving.

Nutritional Value (Amount per Serving):

Calories: 395; Fat: 17.51; Carb: 20.19; Protein: 38.29

Shredded Chicken Gyros

Prep Time: 20 Minutes   Cook Time: 3 Hours   Serves: 8

Ingredients:

- 2 medium onions, chopped
- 6 garlic cloves, minced
- 1 teaspoon lemon-pepper seasoning
- 1 teaspoon dried oregano
- 1/2 teaspoon ground allspice
- 1/2 cup water
- 1/2 cup lemon juice
- 1/4 cup red wine vinegar
- 2 tablespoons olive oil
- 2 pounds boneless skinless chicken breasts
- 8 whole pita breads

- Optional toppings: Tzatziki sauce, torn romaine, and sliced tomato, cucumber and onion

Directions:

1. In a slow cooker, combine first 9 ingredients; add chicken. Cook, covered, on low 3-4 hours or until chicken is tender (a thermometer should read at least 165°).
2. Remove chicken from slow cooker. Shred with 2 forks; return to slow cooker. Using tongs, place chicken mixture on pita breads. Serve with toppings as desired.

Nutritional Value (Amount per Serving):

Calories: 262; Fat: 7.18; Carb: 20; Protein: 29.18

Slow-Cooked Moroccan Chicken

Prep Time: 20 Minutes   Cook Time: 6 Hours   Serves: 4

Ingredients:

- 4 medium carrots, sliced
- 2 large onions, halved and sliced
- 1 broiler/fryer chicken (3 to 4 pounds), cut up, skin removed
- 1/2 teaspoon salt
- 1/2 cup chopped dried apricots
- 1/2 cup raisins
- 1 can (14-1/2 ounces) reduced-sodium chicken broth
- 1/4 cup tomato paste
- 2 tablespoons all-purpose flour
- 2 tablespoons lemon juice
- 2 garlic cloves, minced
- 1-1/2 teaspoons ground ginger
- 1-1/2 teaspoons ground cumin
- 1 teaspoon ground cinnamon
- 3/4 teaspoon pepper
- Hot cooked couscous

Directions:

1. Place carrots and onions in a greased slow cooker. Sprinkle chicken with salt; add to slow cooker.
2. Top with apricots and raisins. In a small bowl, whisk broth, tomato paste, flour, lemon juice, garlic and seasonings until blended; add to slow cooker.
3. Cook, covered, on low until chicken is tender, 6-7 hours.
4. Serve with hot cooked couscous.

Nutritional Value (Amount per Serving):

Calories: 366; Fat: 6.16; Carb: 36.7; Protein: 41.6

Slow-Cooked Lemon Chicken

Prep Time: 20 Minutes Cook Time: 5 Hours 15 Minutes Serves: 6

Ingredients:

- 6 bone-in chicken breast halves (12 ounces each), skin removed
- 1 teaspoon dried oregano
- 1/2 teaspoon seasoned salt
- 1/4 teaspoon pepper
- 2 tablespoons butter
- 1/4 cup water
- 3 tablespoons lemon juice
- 2 garlic cloves, minced
- 1 teaspoon chicken bouillon granules
- 2 teaspoons minced fresh parsley
- Hot cooked rice

Directions:

1. Pat chicken dry with paper towels. Combine the oregano, seasoned salt and pepper; rub over chicken. In a skillet over medium heat, brown the chicken in butter; transfer to a slow cooker.
2. Add water, lemon juice, garlic and bouillon to the skillet; bring to a boil, stirring to loosen browned bits. Pour over chicken.
3. Cover and cook on low for 5-6 hours. Baste chicken with cooking juices. Add parsley.
4. Cover and cook 15-30 minutes longer or until meat juices run clear.
5. Serve with rice. If desired, cooking juices may be thickened before serving.

Nutritional Value (Amount per Serving):

Calories: 749; Fat: 35.73; Carb: 8.11; Protein: 93.2

Slow-Cooked Greek Chicken Dinner

Prep Time: 25 Minutes Cook Time: 5 Hours Serves: 6

Ingredients:

- 6 medium Yukon Gold potatoes, quartered
- 1 broiler/fryer chicken (3-1/2 pounds), cut up and skin removed
- 2 large onions, quartered

- 1 whole garlic bulb, separated and peeled
- 3 teaspoons dried oregano
- 1 teaspoon salt
- 3/4 teaspoon pepper
- 1/2 cup plus 1 tablespoon water, divided
- 1 tablespoon olive oil
- 4 teaspoons cornstarch

Directions:

1. Place potatoes in a slow cooker. Add chicken, onions and garlic; sprinkle with seasonings. Pour 1/2 cup water over top.
2. Drizzle with oil. Cook, covered, on low until chicken and vegetables are tender, 5-6 hours.
3. In a bowl, mix cornstarch and remaining water until smooth. Remove chicken and vegetables from slow cooker; keep warm.
4. Strain cooking juices into a small saucepan; skim fat. Bring juices to a boil.
5. Stir cornstarch mixture; stir into juices. Bring to a boil; cook and stir until thickened, 1-2 minutes.
6. Serve with chicken and vegetables.

Nutritional Value (Amount per Serving):

Calories: 474; Fat: 6.07; Carb: 73.57; Protein: 31.99

Herbed Slow-Cooker Chicken

Prep Time: 5 Minutes Cook Time: 4 Hours Serves: 4

Ingredients:

- 1 tablespoon olive oil
- 1 teaspoon paprika
- 1/2 teaspoon garlic powder
- 1/2 teaspoon seasoned salt
- 1/2 teaspoon dried thyme
- 1/2 teaspoon dried basil
- 1/2 teaspoon pepper
- 1/2 teaspoon browning sauce, optional
- 4 bone-in chicken breast halves (8 ounces each)
- 1/2 cup chicken broth

Directions:

1. In a small bowl, combine the first 7 ingredients and, if desired, browning sauce; rub over chicken.
2. Place in a slow cooker; add broth. Cook, covered, on low until chicken is tender, 4-5 hours.

Nutritional Value (Amount per Serving):

Calories: 308; Fat: 9.89; Carb: 8.41; Protein: 46.33

Chunky Chicken Cacciatore

Prep Time: 10 Minutes Cook Time: 4 Hours Serves: 6

Ingredients:

- 6 boneless skinless chicken thighs (about 1-1/2 pounds)
- 2 medium zucchini, cut into 1-inch slices
- 1 medium green pepper, cut into 1-inch pieces
- 1 large sweet onion, coarsely chopped
- 1/2 teaspoon dried oregano
- 1 jar (24 ounces) garden-style spaghetti sauce
- Hot cooked spaghetti
- Optional: Sliced ripe olives and shredded Parmesan cheese

Directions:

1. Place chicken and vegetables in a slow cooker; sprinkle with oregano. Pour sauce over top.
2. Cook, covered, on low 4-5 hours or until chicken is tender.
3. Remove chicken; break up slightly with 2 forks.
4. Return to slow cooker. Serve with spaghetti. If desired, top with olives and cheese.

Nutritional Value (Amount per Serving):

Calories: 250; Fat: 5.11; Carb: 20.76; Protein: 29.81

Crock Pot BBQ Chicken

Prep Time: 5 Minutes Cook Time: 3 Hours Serves: 4

Ingredients:

- 1½ cups BBQ sauce
- ¼ cup apple cider vinegar
- 2 tablespoons brown sugar
- ½ teaspoon onion powder
- ½ teaspoon garlic powder
- 2 pounds boneless, skinless chicken breasts

Directions:

1. In a bowl, whisk the BBQ sauce, apple cider vinegar, brown sugar, onion powder, and garlic powder together.
2. Place the chicken breasts in the bottom of the slow cooker.
3. Pour the sauce over the chicken breasts, covering them fully.

4. Cook the chicken on high for 2-3 hours or on low for 4-6 hours.
5. Shred the chicken directly in the slow cooker or remove to shred and return to the sauce.
6. Give the chicken a good stir to coat it in the sauce.

Nutritional Value (Amount per Serving):

Calories: 489; Fat: 13.1; Carb: 70.92; Protein: 22.66

Slow Cooker Lemon Garlic Chicken

Prep Time: 15 Minutes   Cook Time: 3 Hours 15 Minutes   Serves: 6

Ingredients:

- 1 teaspoon dried oregano
- ½ teaspoon salt
- ¼ teaspoon ground black pepper
- 2 tablespoons butter
- 2 pounds skinless, boneless chicken breast halves
- ¼ cup water
- 3 tablespoons fresh lemon juice
- 2 cloves garlic, minced
- 1 teaspoon chicken bouillon granules
- 1 teaspoon chopped fresh parsley

Directions:

1. Mix together oregano, salt, and pepper in a small bowl. Rub spice mixture all over chicken breasts. Melt butter in a skillet over medium heat.
2. Cook chicken in butter until lightly browned, 3 to 5 minutes per side.
3. Place chicken in a slow cooker.
4. Mix water, lemon juice, garlic, and bouillon in the same skillet; bring to boil.
5. Pour mixture over chicken in the slow cooker.
6. Cover and cook on Low for 6 hours or on High for 3 hours. Add parsley to the slow cooker 15 to 30 minutes before the end of cook time.
7. Serve hot and enjoy!

Nutritional Value (Amount per Serving):

Calories: 396; Fat: 12.13; Carb: 1.17; Protein: 66.53

Crock Pot Turkey Chili

Prep Time: 20 Minutes   Cook Time: 6 Hours   Serves: 6

Ingredients:

- 1 lb ground turkey
- 1 onion, chopped
- 1 red bell pepper, chopped
- 2 cloves garlic, minced
- 1 can (15 oz) kidney beans, drained and rinsed
- 1 can (15 oz) black beans, drained and rinsed
- 1 can (15 oz) diced tomatoes
- 1 can (6 oz) tomato paste
- 1 cup chicken broth
- 2 tablespoons chili powder
- 1 teaspoon ground cumin
- 1 teaspoon paprika
- 1/2 teaspoon cayenne pepper (adjust to taste)
- Salt and pepper to taste
- Shredded cheddar cheese and sour cream for topping (optional)

Directions:

1. In a skillet, cook ground turkey over medium heat until browned. Drain excess fat.
2. Place cooked turkey, chopped onion, chopped red bell pepper, and minced garlic in the crock pot.
3. Add kidney beans, black beans, diced tomatoes, tomato paste, chicken broth, chili powder, ground cumin, paprika, cayenne pepper, salt, and pepper to the crock pot. Stir to combine.
4. Cover and cook on low for 6 hours.
5. Serve with shredded cheddar cheese and sour cream if desired.

Nutritional Value (Amount per Serving):

Calories: 359; Fat: 12.29; Carb: 30.93; Protein: 33.74

Crock Pot Chicken Tikka Masala

Prep Time: 20 Minutes   Cook Time: 5 Hours   Serves: 4

Ingredients:

- 4 boneless, skinless chicken breasts, cut into bite-sized pieces
- 1 onion, finely chopped
- 3 cloves garlic, minced
- 1 can (14 oz) diced tomatoes
- 1/2 cup plain yogurt
- 2 tablespoons tomato paste
- 2 teaspoons garam masala

- 1 teaspoon ground cumin
- 1 teaspoon ground coriander
- 1 teaspoon paprika
- 1/2 teaspoon turmeric
- Salt and pepper to taste
- 1/2 cup heavy cream
- Fresh cilantro for garnish (optional)
- Cooked rice for serving

Directions:

1. Place chicken pieces and chopped onion in the crock pot.
2. In a separate bowl, mix together minced garlic, diced tomatoes, plain yogurt, tomato paste, garam masala, ground cumin, ground coriander, paprika, turmeric, salt, and pepper.
3. Pour the tomato mixture over the chicken and onions.
4. Cover and cook on low for 5 hours.
5. Stir in heavy cream before serving.
6. Garnish with fresh cilantro and serve with cooked rice.

Nutritional Value (Amount per Serving):

Calories: 511; Fat: 20.01; Carb: 59.04; Protein: 24.27

Crock Pot Chicken Fajitas

Prep Time: 15 Minutes Cook Time: 4 Hours Serves: 4

Ingredients:

- 1.5 lbs boneless, skinless chicken breasts
- 1 onion, thinly sliced
- 1 red bell pepper, thinly sliced
- 1 green bell pepper, thinly sliced
- 1 can (14 oz) diced tomatoes with green chilies
- 1 packet (1.25 oz) fajita seasoning mix
- 2 tablespoons lime juice
- Flour tortillas for serving
- Sour cream, salsa, and shredded cheese for topping (optional)

Directions:

1. Place chicken breasts in the bottom of the crock pot.
2. Add sliced onion, red bell pepper, and green bell pepper on top of the chicken.
3. Sprinkle the fajita seasoning mix over the ingredients.
4. Pour diced tomatoes with green chilies and lime juice over the top.
5. Cover and cook on low for 4 hours.

6. Shred the chicken using two forks.
7. Serve the chicken and vegetable mixture in flour tortillas.
8. Top with sour cream, salsa, and shredded cheese if desired.

Nutritional Value (Amount per Serving):

Calories: 427; Fat: 14.82; Carb: 51.33; Protein: 20.42

Slow Cooker Teriyaki Chicken

Prep Time: 10 Minutes Cook Time: 4 Hours 10 Minutes Serves: 6

Ingredients:

- 1 1/2 pounds boneless skinless chicken breasts
- 2 teaspoons garlic minced
- 2 teaspoons ginger minced
- 1/4 cup honey
- 3 tablespoons brown sugar
- 1/2 cup low sodium soy sauce
- 2 teaspoons toasted sesame oil
- 2 tablespoons rice vinegar
- 1/4 cup cold water
- 2 tablespoons cornstarch
- 1 tablespoon sesame seeds
- 2 tablespoons sliced green onions

Directions:

1. Place the chicken breasts in a slow cooker.
2. In a small bowl, whisk together the garlic, ginger, honey, brown sugar, soy sauce sesame oil and rice vinegar.
3. Pour the soy sauce mixture over the chicken.
4. Cover and cook on HIGH for 3-4 hours or on LOW for 6-7 hours.
5. Remove the chicken from the slow cooker and shred with two forks.
6. Pour the teriyaki sauce from the slow cooker through a strainer into a saucepan.
7. Place the saucepan on the stove over medium high heat and bring to a simmer.
8. In a small bowl, mix the cornstarch with the water until dissolved.
9. Pour the cornstarch into the pan and bring a boil. Cook for 1-2 minutes or until sauce has just thickened.
10. Pour the sauce over the shredded chicken and toss to coat the chicken. Sprinkle with sesame seeds and green onions, then serve.

Nutritional Value (Amount per Serving):

Calories: 245; Fat: 5.37; Carb: 20.92; Protein: 27.86

Slow Cooker Orange Chicken

Prep Time: 20 Minutes   Cook Time: 3 Hours   Serves: 6

Ingredients:

- 2 pounds boneless skinless chicken breasts or tenders cut into bite size pieces
- 1/3 cup cornstarch
- 4 tablespoons olive oil
- 1 1/2 cups orange marmalade
- 1/2 cup low sodium soy sauce
- 2 tablespoons vinegar
- 1 teaspoon sesame oil
- 1 teaspoon ground ginger
- 3 cloves garlic minced
- 1/2 teaspoon
- 1 teaspoon sesame seeds more for garnish
- scallions for garnish

Directions:

1. Cut the chicken into approximately 1" pieces.
2. Pour the cornstarch into a shallow dish, add the chicken, and toss to evenly coat.
3. Heat the oil in a large skillet over medium high heat and add the coated chicken. Lightly brown on each side, not cooking thoroughly.
4. Transfer the browned chicken into the basin of a slow cooker.
5. In a medium bowl, whisk together the marmalade, soy sauce, vinegar, sesame oil, ginger, garlic, red pepper flakes and sesame seeds.
6. Pour the sauce over the chicken.
7. Stir everything to combine.
8. Cover and cook on LOW for 3 hours. Check and stir halfway through to make sure it isn't burning.
9. Garnish with chopped scallions and a sprinkle of sesame seeds.
10. Serve over rice.

Nutritional Value (Amount per Serving):

Calories: 711; Fat: 29.61; Carb: 88.19; Protein: 27.16

Chicken and Sausage Gumbo

Prep Time: 20 Minutes   Cook Time: 6 Hours   Serves: 6

Ingredients:

- 4 boneless, skinless chicken thighs, cut into bite-sized pieces
- 1 lb Andouille sausage, sliced
- 1 onion, chopped
- 1 green bell pepper, chopped
- 1 red bell pepper, chopped

- 3 stalks celery, chopped
- 4 cloves garlic, minced
- 1 can (14 oz) diced tomatoes
- 4 cups chicken broth
- 2 teaspoons gumbo file powder (optional)
- 1 teaspoon dried thyme
- 1 teaspoon paprika
- 1/2 teaspoon cayenne pepper (adjust to taste)
- Salt and pepper to taste
- Cooked white rice for serving
- Chopped green onions for garnish (optional)

Directions:

1. Place chicken pieces, sliced Andouille sausage, chopped onion, chopped green bell pepper, chopped red bell pepper, chopped celery, minced garlic, diced tomatoes, chicken broth, gumbo file powder (if using), dried thyme, paprika, cayenne pepper, salt, and pepper in the crock pot.
2. Cover and cook on low for 6 hours.
3. Serve the chicken and sausage gumbo over cooked white rice.
4. Garnish with chopped green onions if desired.

Nutritional Value (Amount per Serving):

Calories: 758; Fat: 33.74; Carb: 51.06; Protein: 64.23

Chapter 4: Beef, Pork and Lamb

Mediterranean Pork Souvlaki

Prep Time: 15 Minutes   Cook Time: 4 Hours   Serves: 5

Ingredients:

- 2 pounds pork shoulder, cubed
- 1 red bell pepper, sliced
- 1 yellow bell pepper, sliced
- 1 red onion, sliced
- 4 cloves garlic, minced
- 1/4 cup olive oil
- 1/4 cup lemon juice
- 2 teaspoons dried oregano
- Salt and pepper to taste
- Wooden skewers, soaked in water

Directions:

1. In a bowl, combine pork, bell peppers, red onion, and garlic.
2. In a separate bowl, whisk together olive oil, lemon juice, oregano, salt, and pepper.
3. Pour the marinade over the pork mixture and toss to coat evenly. Let it marinate for 1 hour.
4. Thread the marinated pork and vegetables onto the soaked skewers.
5. Place skewers in the crock pot and cook on low for 4 hours.
6. Serve with pita bread and tzatziki.

Nutritional Value (Amount per Serving):

Calories: 599; Fat: 43.01; Carb: 4.63; Protein: 46.28

Slow Cooked Mediterranean Beef Stroganoff

Prep Time: 15 Minutes   Cook Time: 8 Hours   Serves: 6

Ingredients:

- 2 pounds beef stew meat, cubed
- 1 onion, finely chopped
- 8 oz mushrooms, sliced
- 3 cloves garlic, minced
- 1 cup beef broth
- 1/2 cup dry red wine
- 2 tablespoons tomato paste
- 1 teaspoon dried thyme
- 1 teaspoon paprika
- 1 cup sour cream
- Salt and pepper to taste
- Fresh parsley for garnish

Directions:

1. In a crock pot, combine beef, onion, mushrooms, and garlic.
2. In a bowl, mix beef broth, red wine, tomato paste, thyme, paprika, salt, and pepper. Pour over the beef mixture.
3. Cover and cook on low for 8 hours.
4. Stir in sour cream just before serving.
5. Garnish with fresh parsley and serve over egg noodles or rice.

Nutritional Value (Amount per Serving):

Calories: 325; Fat: 17.29; Carb: 41.17; Protein: 6.41

Mediterranean Lamb and Chickpea Tagine

Prep Time: 20 Minutes Cook Time: 6 Hours Serves: 5

Ingredients:

- 2 pounds lamb shoulder, cubed
- 1 can (15 oz) chickpeas, drained and rinsed
- 2 large carrots, sliced
- 1 onion, chopped
- 3 cloves garlic, minced
- 1 teaspoon ground cumin
- 1 teaspoon ground coriander
- 1 teaspoon ground cinnamon
- 1 cup chicken broth
- 1/2 cup dried apricots, chopped
- Salt and pepper to taste
- Fresh cilantro for garnish

Directions:

1. Brown lamb in a skillet over medium-high heat; transfer to the crock pot.
2. Add chickpeas, carrots, onion, and garlic to the crock pot.
3. In a bowl, mix cumin, coriander, cinnamon, salt, and pepper. Sprinkle over the lamb and vegetables.
4. Pour in chicken broth and add dried apricots.
5. Cover and cook on low for 6 hours.
6. Garnish with fresh cilantro before serving.

Nutritional Value (Amount per Serving):

Calories: 475; Fat: 19.85; Carb: 24.36; Protein: 50.82

Mediterranean Pork and Olive Ragout

Prep Time: 15 Minutes Cook Time: 7 Hours Serves: 6

Ingredients:

- 2 pounds pork loin, cubed
- 1 cup Kalamata olives, pitted
- 1 can (14 oz) diced tomatoes
- 1 onion, finely chopped
- 4 cloves garlic, minced
- 1/2 cup dry white wine
- 2 tablespoons capers
- 1 teaspoon dried rosemary

- 1 teaspoon dried thyme
- Salt and pepper to taste

Directions:

1. In the crock pot, combine pork, olives, diced tomatoes, onion, and garlic.
2. Pour in white wine and add capers, rosemary, thyme, salt, and pepper.
3. Stir well and cook on low for 7 hours.
4. Adjust seasoning if needed and serve over couscous or mashed potatoes.

Nutritional Value (Amount per Serving):

Calories: 387; Fat: 21.24; Carb: 5.95; Protein: 41.7

Greek-Style Slow Cooked Beef Gyros

Prep Time: 15 Minutes Cook Time: 6 Hours Serves: 5

Ingredients:

- 2 pounds beef sirloin, thinly sliced
- 1 large red onion, thinly sliced
- 1 cup cherry tomatoes, halved
- 4 cloves garlic, minced
- 1/4 cup olive oil
- 1/4 cup red wine vinegar
- 1 tablespoon dried oregano
- 1 teaspoon ground cumin
- 1 teaspoon smoked paprika
- Salt and pepper to taste
- Pita bread and Tzatziki for serving

Directions:

1. In a bowl, combine beef, red onion, cherry tomatoes, and garlic.
2. In a separate bowl, whisk together olive oil, red wine vinegar, oregano, cumin, paprika, salt, and pepper.
3. Pour the marinade over the beef mixture and toss to coat evenly. Let it marinate for 1 hour.
4. Transfer the marinated mixture to the crock pot.
5. Cover and cook on low for 6 hours. Stir occasionally.
6. Serve the beef gyro mixture in warm pita bread with a generous dollop of Tzatziki.

Nutritional Value (Amount per Serving):

Calories: 576; Fat: 39.6; Carb: 9.63; Protein: 44.02

Mediterranean Beef and Rice

Prep Time: 10 Minutes Cook Time: 8 Hours Serves: 12

Ingredients:

- 1 ½ tablespoons Garam Masala Spice
- 1 tablespoon Beef Bouillon Granules

- 1 teaspoon Mediterranean Spiced Sea Salt
- 1 teaspoon Seasoned Salt
- ½ teaspoon Ground Turmeric
- ½ teaspoon Freshly Ground Black Pepper
- ½ teaspoon Ground Cinnamon
- ½ teaspoon Ground Ginger
- 3 pounds Beef Pot Roast (cut into small pieces, or use beef stew meat)
- 16 ounces Frozen Mixed Vegetables (or substitute fresh vegetables)
- 3 cloves Garlic (minced)
- 2 cups Water
- 1 cup Pine Nuts (toasted)
- 2 cups Rice (for serving)

Directions:

1. In a small mixing bowl, combine together the garam masala, beef bouillon granules, sea salt, season all, turmeric, black pepper, cinnamon and ginger.
2. Toss meat with spices.
3. Add seasoned meat, water, vegetables and minced garlic to a 6 quart or larger slow cooker.
4. Cover and cook on LOW for 8 hours.
5. Before serving, mix in toasted pine nuts
6. Serve over rice.

Nutritional Value (Amount per Serving):

Calories: 337; Fat: 19.61; Carb: 17.59; Protein: 30.07

Slow-cooker beef goulash

Prep Time: 25 Minutes Cook Time: 7 Hours Serves: 8

Ingredients:

- 3 tbsp olive oil
- 2kg braising or stewing steak, cut into chunks
- 2 large onions, finely chopped
- 4 mixed peppers, cut into 4cm chunks
- 3 garlic cloves, crushed
- 2 tbsp flour
- 2 tsp caraway seeds
- 2 tsp hot smoked paprika
- 1 tbsp sweet smoked paprika, plus extra to serve
- 4 tbsp tomato purée
- 4 large tomatoes cut into small chunks
- 400-500ml beef stock

- 300ml soured cream
- small bunch of parsley, chopped

Directions:

1. Heat the slow cooker to low and heat 2 tbsp oil in a deep frying pan over a medium heat. Season and sear the beef in batches until brown on all sides. Transfer to a plate.
2. Put the remaining oil in the pan and fry the onions for 10 minutes until lightly golden. Add the peppers and garlic, and fry for another 5-10 minutes, then stir in the flour and all of the spices. Cook for 2 more minutes, then stir in the tomato purée, tomatoes and 400ml beef stock. Season well. Bring the mixture to a simmer, then tip into the slow cooker with the seared beef. Add the remaining stock, if needed, to cover the meat completely. Cover and cook for 6-7 hours until the beef is tender and the sauce has thickened slightly.
3. Season to taste, then swirl the soured cream and most of the parsley through the stew. Scatter over the remaining parsley and some sweet smoked paprika, then serve with small roasted potatoes or brown rice, if you like.

Nutritional Value (Amount per Serving):

Calories: 518; Fat: 19.23; Carb: 76.62; Protein: 11.59

Pineapple-Pork Tacos

Prep Time: 20 Minutes Cook Time: 7 Hours Serves: 6

Ingredients:

- 1 lb boneless pork shoulder roast, trimmed
- 1 package (1 oz) taco seasoning mix
- 1 can (8 oz) pineapple tidbits in juice, drained
- 2 teaspoons lime juice
- 1 box (4.6 oz) Crunchy Taco Shells (12 Count)
- 3/4 cup shredded Cheddar cheese (3 oz)
- 1 1/2 cups shredded lettuce
- 3/4 cup chopped tomato
- 1/3 cup sour cream
- 1/3 cup salsa

Directions:

1. Spray a slow cooker with cooking spray. Place pork in slow cooker; sprinkle with taco seasoning mix.
2. Cover; cook on Low heat setting 7 to 9 hours or until pork pulls apart easily with fork.

3. Remove pork from slow cooker; shred pork. Stir into liquid in slow cooker. Stir in pineapple and lime juice.
4. To serve, divide pork among taco shells (about 1/4 cup each), and top with remaining ingredients.

Nutritional Value (Amount per Serving):

Calories: 200; Fat: 6.28; Carb: 14.64; Protein: 20.36

Beef and Spinach Lasagna

Prep Time: 30 Minutes Cook Time: 4-6 Hours Serves: 6

Ingredients:

- 1 pound ground beef
- 1 onion, chopped
- 2 cloves garlic, minced
- 1 can (28 ounces) crushed tomatoes
- 1 can (6 ounces) tomato paste
- 1 teaspoon dried basil
- 1 teaspoon dried oregano
- Salt and black pepper to taste
- 8 lasagna noodles, cooked and drained
- 1 1/2 cups ricotta cheese
- 2 cups shredded mozzarella cheese
- 2 cups fresh spinach leaves
- Grated Parmesan cheese for topping
- Fresh basil leaves for garnish (optional)

Directions

1. In a skillet, brown the ground beef with chopped onion and minced garlic. Drain any excess fat.
2. Stir in crushed tomatoes, tomato paste, dried basil, dried oregano, salt, and black pepper.
3. In the crock pot, layer some of the meat sauce, followed by a layer of cooked lasagna noodles, a layer of ricotta cheese, a layer of shredded mozzarella cheese, and a layer of fresh spinach leaves. Repeat the layers.
4. Top with a final layer of meat sauce and sprinkle with grated Parmesan cheese.
5. Cover and cook on low for 4-6 hours or until the lasagna is hot and bubbly.
6. Serve hot, garnished with fresh basil leaves if desired.

Nutritional Value (Amount per Serving):

Calories: 3922; Fat: 136.4; Carb: 449.64; Protein: 233.08

Lamb and Bean Stew

Prep Time: 15 Minutes   Cook Time: 3 Hours   Serves: 6

Ingredients:

- ½ lb of lamb stew meat
- 1 lb pre-soaked pinto beans
- 8-10 medium red potatoes
- 4 medium carrots
- 2 large Spanish onions
- 1 celery heart
- 1 large zucchini
- ¾ cup soy sauce
- garlic powder

Directions:

1. After spraying your slow cooker with oil add diced onions, sliced carrots and celery.
2. Add your beans. If you are running short on time, or do not have pre-soaked beans, you can use low sodium white beans.
3. Add Lamb stew meat.
4. Top with diced zucchini and red potatoes.
5. Cover with soy sauce and water. Cook for 3 hours on high.
6. Serve hot!

Nutritional Value (Amount per Serving):

Calories: 681; Fat: 10.92; Carb: 124.44; Protein: 25.45

Teriyaki Beef and Broccoli

Prep Time: 20 Minutes   Cook Time: 6 Hours   Serves: 4

Ingredients:

- 2 cups beef broth
- ½ cup low-sodium soy sauce
- ⅓ cup packed brown sugar
- 1 ½ teaspoon sesame oil
- 1 clove garlic minced
- 1 ½ lb beef top sirloin steak sliced into ½ inch thick strips
- 2 tablespoon corn starch
- ¼ cup cold water
- 4 cups broccoli florets steamed

Directions:

1. Combine the first 5 ingredients in a slow cooker.
2. Add beef and stir to coat. Cover.
3. Set slow cooker on low and cook until tender. 6 hours on low or 4 hours on high.

4. In a small bowl whisk together cornstarch and water until smooth. Add to hot liquid in slow cooker and stir.
5. Cover and cook until teriyaki sauce has thickened, about 30 minutes.
6. Serve over hot rice and topped with steamed broccoli.
7. Garnish with sliced green onions and sesame seeds if desired.

Nutritional Value (Amount per Serving):

Calories: 498; Fat: 21.3; Carb: 35.2; Protein: 40.62

Pork and Sweet Corn Chowder

Prep Time: 15 Minutes   Cook Time: 6-8 Hours   Serves: 4

Ingredients:

- 2 pounds pork baby back ribs
- 1 cup blackberry jam
- 1/2 cup BBQ sauce
- 1/4 cup apple cider vinegar
- 2 cloves garlic, minced
- Salt and black pepper to taste

Directions:

1. Season the pork baby back ribs with salt and black pepper.
2. Place the ribs in the crock pot.
3. In a bowl, mix blackberry jam, BBQ sauce, apple cider vinegar, and minced garlic.
4. Pour the sauce mixture over the ribs in the crock pot.
5. Cover and cook on low for 6-8 hours or until the ribs are tender and cooked through.
6. Serve hot.

Nutritional Value (Amount per Serving):

Calories: 583; Fat: 35.87; Carb: 20.73; Protein: 46.38

Slow Cooker Beef Curry

Prep Time: 15 Minutes   Cook Time: 8 Hours   Serves: 6

Ingredients:

- 1 (14.5 ounce) can diced tomatoes, undrained
- 1 large onion, sliced
- 1 cup beef broth
- 1 cup coconut milk
- 3 tablespoons curry powder
- 3 cloves garlic, pressed
- 2 bay leaves

- 1 teaspoon minced fresh ginger root
- 1 teaspoon cayenne pepper, or more to taste (Optional)
- 1 whole star anise
- salt and ground black pepper to taste
- 1 (1 1/2-pound) flank steak
- ½ lime, juiced

Directions:

1. Combine diced tomatoes with their juices, onion, beef broth, coconut milk, curry powder, garlic, bay leaves, ginger, cayenne pepper, star anise, salt, and pepper in the bottom of a slow cooker. Stir to combine. Add flank steak to the mixture.
2. Cover and cook on Low until beef are tender and cooked through, about 8 hours. Add lime juice just prior to serving.

Nutritional Value (Amount per Serving):

Calories: 181; Fat: 11.72; Carb: 12.93; Protein: 8.69

Pork and Pumpkin Chili

Prep Time: 20 Minutes Cook Time: 6-8 Hours Serves: 6

Ingredients:

- 2 pounds ground pork
- 1 onion, chopped
- 2 cloves garlic, minced
- 1 can (14 ounces) diced tomatoes
- 1 can (14 ounces) pumpkin puree
- 2 cans (15 ounces each) black beans, drained and rinsed
- 1 can (4 ounces) diced green chilies
- 2 tablespoons chili powder
- 1 teaspoon ground cumin
- 1/2 teaspoon ground cinnamon
- 1/2 teaspoon ground nutmeg
- Salt and black pepper to taste
- Shredded cheddar cheese, chopped green onions, and sour cream for garnish (optional)

Directions:

1. In a skillet, brown the ground pork over medium-high heat, breaking it into crumbles. Drain any excess fat.
2. Transfer the cooked pork to the crock pot.
3. Add chopped onions, minced garlic, diced tomatoes, pumpkin puree, black beans, diced green chilies, chili powder, cumin, ground cinnamon, ground

nutmeg, salt, and black pepper.
4. Stir to combine all ingredients.
5. Cover and cook on low for 6-8 hours.
6. Serve hot, garnished with shredded cheddar cheese, chopped green onions, and sour cream if desired.

Nutritional Value (Amount per Serving):

Calories: 1053; Fat: 65.62; Carb: 50.18; Protein: 72.85

Beef and Quinoa Stuffed Bell Peppers

Prep Time: 30 Minutes Cook Time: 4-6 Hours Serves: 6

Ingredients:

- 6 bell peppers, tops removed, seeds and membranes removed
- 1 pound ground beef
- 1 onion, chopped
- 1 can (14 ounces) diced tomatoes
- 1 cup cooked quinoa
- 1/2 cup corn kernels
- 1/2 cup black beans, drained and rinsed
- 1/2 teaspoon chili powder
- 1/2 teaspoon cumin
- Salt and black pepper to taste
- Shredded cheddar cheese for topping

Directions:

1. In a skillet, brown the ground beef with chopped onion. Drain any excess fat.
2. In a bowl, mix the cooked ground beef and onion with diced tomatoes, cooked quinoa, corn kernels, black beans, chili powder, cumin, salt, and black pepper.
3. Stuff the bell peppers with the mixture and place them in the crock pot.
4. Cover and cook on low for 4-6 hours, or until the bell peppers are tender.
5. Sprinkle shredded cheddar cheese on top of each stuffed bell pepper before serving.

Nutritional Value (Amount per Serving):

Calories: 299; Fat: 13.67; Carb: 20.37; Protein: 24.07

Lamb and Potato Casserole

Prep Time: 20 Minutes Cook Time: 6-7 Hours Serves: 6

Ingredients:

- 2 pounds boneless lamb stew meat, cubed
- 4 potatoes, peeled and cubed
- 2 onions, chopped
- 2 cloves garlic, minced
- 1 cup beef broth
- 1/4 cup red wine
- 2 teaspoons dried rosemary
- 1 teaspoon dried thyme
- Salt and black pepper to taste
- Chopped fresh parsley for garnish (optional)

Directions:

1. Place lamb stew meat, cubed potatoes, chopped onions, minced garlic, beef broth, red wine, dried rosemary, dried thyme, salt, and black pepper in the crock pot.
2. Stir to combine all ingredients.
3. Cover and cook on low for 6-7 hours or until lamb is tender and potatoes are cooked through.
4. Serve hot, garnished with chopped fresh parsley if desired.

Nutritional Value (Amount per Serving):

Calories: 440; Fat: 8; Carb: 54.33; Protein: 36.96

Slow-Cooker Apricot-Glazed Pork Roast and Stuffing

Prep Time: 10 Minutes Cook Time: 7 Hours Serves: 6

Ingredients:

- 4 cups herb-seasoned stuffing cubes
- 3/4 cup chicken broth (from 32-oz carton)
- 1/2 cup dried apricots, chopped
- 1/3 cup frozen chopped onions (from 14-oz bag)
- 1 boneless pork loin roast (2 to 2 1/2 lb), trimmed of fat
- 1/3 cup apricot jam
- 1 tablespoon balsamic vinegar

Directions:

1. Spray slow cooker with cooking spray. In cooker, mix stuffing, broth, apricots and onions. Place pork on stuffing mixture. In small bowl, mix jam and vinegar; brush over pork.
2. Cover and cook on Low heat setting 7 to 8 hours.
3. Remove pork from cooker; place on cutting board. Stir stuffing before

serving. Cut pork into slices; serve with stuffing.

Nutritional Value (Amount per Serving):

Calories: 898; Fat: 17.03; Carb: 72.48; Protein: 93.08

Slow-Cooker Beef and Bean Burritos

Prep Time: 20 Minutes Cook Time: 6-7 Hours Serves: 6

Ingredients:

- 2 pounds beef stew meat, cubed
- 1 onion, chopped
- 1 can (14 ounces) diced tomatoes
- 1 can (14 ounces) pinto beans, drained and rinsed
- 1 can (4 ounces) diced green chilies
- 1 tablespoon chili powder
- 1 teaspoon cumin
- 1/2 teaspoon garlic powder
- Salt and black pepper to taste
- Flour tortillas for serving
- Shredded lettuce, diced tomatoes, shredded cheese, and sour cream for toppings

Directions:

1. Place beef stew meat, chopped onion, diced tomatoes, pinto beans, diced green chilies, chili powder, cumin, garlic powder, salt, and black pepper in the crock pot.
2. Stir to combine all ingredients.
3. Cover and cook on low for 6-7 hours or until beef is tender.
4. Serve the beef and bean mixture in flour tortillas and top with shredded lettuce, diced tomatoes, shredded cheese, and sour cream.

Nutritional Value (Amount per Serving):

Calories: 266; Fat: 14.01; Carb: 21.19; Protein: 5.43

Chapter 5: Fish and Seafood

Mediterranean Garlic Lemon Shrimp

Prep Time: 15 Minutes   Cook Time: 2 Hours   Serves: 4-6

Ingredients:

- 1.5 lbs large shrimp, peeled and deveined
- 4 cloves garlic, minced
- 1/4 cup fresh parsley, chopped
- 1/3 cup olive oil
- 1/4 cup fresh lemon juice
- 1 teaspoon dried oregano
- Salt and pepper to taste

Directions:

1. In a bowl, mix together garlic, parsley, olive oil, lemon juice, oregano, salt, and pepper.
2. Place the shrimp in the crock pot and pour the mixture over them, ensuring they are well-coated.
3. Cover and cook on low for 2 hours, stirring occasionally.
4. Serve over cooked rice or with crusty bread to soak up the delicious sauce.

Nutritional Value (Amount per Serving):

Calories: 154; Fat: 14.57; Carb: 5.75; Protein: 1.29

Mediterranean Herb-Roasted Cod

Prep Time: 20 Minutes   Cook Time: 3 Hours   Serves: 4-6

Ingredients:

- 2 lbs cod fillets
- 1/4 cup fresh basil, chopped
- 1/4 cup fresh dill, chopped
- 1/4 cup fresh mint, chopped
- 1/3 cup olive oil
- 3 cloves garlic, minced
- 1 lemon, sliced
- Salt and pepper to taste

Directions:

1. Mix together basil, dill, mint, olive oil, and garlic in a bowl.
2. Place cod fillets in the crock pot, season with salt and pepper, and pour the herb mixture over them.
3. Arrange lemon slices on top, cover, and cook on low for 3 hours.
4. Serve with a side of roasted vegetables or a Greek salad.

Nutritional Value (Amount per Serving):

Calories: 277; Fat: 15.94; Carb: 2.17; Protein: 30.1

Slow-Cooked Mediterranean Cioppino

Prep Time: 30 Minutes   Cook Time: 4 Hours   Serves: 6-8

Ingredients:

- 1 lb mixed seafood (mussels, clams, squid, and shrimp)
- 1 onion, finely chopped
- 2 cloves garlic, minced
- 1 can (28 oz) crushed tomatoes
- 1/2 cup dry white wine
- 1/4 cup fresh basil, chopped
- 1/4 cup fresh parsley, chopped
- 1 teaspoon dried oregano
- Salt and pepper to taste

Directions:

1. In the crock pot, combine chopped onion, minced garlic, crushed tomatoes, white wine, basil, parsley, oregano, salt, and pepper.
2. Add the mixed seafood and stir well.
3. Cover and cook on low for 4 hours or until the seafood is cooked through.
4. Serve in bowls, garnished with additional fresh herbs.

Nutritional Value (Amount per Serving):

Calories: 69; Fat: 1.95; Carb: 10.79; Protein: 2.76

Lemon Garlic Butter Scallops

Prep Time: 15 Minutes   Cook Time: 2 Hours 30 Minutes   Serves: 4-6

Ingredients:

- 1.5 lbs fresh scallops
- 1/2 cup unsalted butter, melted
- 4 cloves garlic, minced
- Zest of 1 lemon
- 1/4 cup fresh parsley, chopped
- Salt and pepper to taste

Directions:

1. Rinse and pat dry the scallops; place them in the crock pot.
2. In a bowl, mix melted butter, minced garlic, lemon zest, parsley, salt, and pepper.
3. Pour the butter mixture over the scallops, ensuring they are evenly coated.
4. Cover and cook on low for 2.5 hours. Serve over a bed of couscous or quinoa.

Nutritional Value (Amount per Serving):

Calories: 216; Fat: 13.09; Carb: 6.82; Protein: 17.61

Mediterranean Lemon Herb Salmon

Prep Time: 15 Minutes Cook Time: 2 Hours 30 Minutes Serves: 4-6

Ingredients:

- 2 lbs salmon fillets
- 1/4 cup fresh dill, chopped
- 1/4 cup fresh parsley, chopped
- 1 lemon, sliced
- 1/3 cup olive oil
- 3 cloves garlic, minced
- 1 teaspoon dried thyme
- Salt and pepper to taste

Directions:

1. Place salmon fillets in the crock pot.
2. In a bowl, mix together dill, parsley, olive oil, minced garlic, dried thyme, salt, and pepper.
3. Pour the herb mixture over the salmon, ensuring it is evenly coated.
4. Arrange lemon slices on top, cover, and cook on low for 2.5 hours or until the salmon is cooked through and flakes easily.
5. Serve with a side of quinoa or roasted vegetables for a complete Mediterranean-inspired meal.

Nutritional Value (Amount per Serving):

Calories: 413; Fat: 27.35; Carb: 2.37; Protein: 37.87

Mediterranean Crock Pot Sardine Stew

Prep Time: 20 Minutes Cook Time: 3 Hours Serves: 6

Ingredients:

- 1 pound fresh sardines, cleaned and scaled
- 1 cup diced onions
- 1 cup diced bell peppers (red and green)
- 1 cup diced zucchini
- 1 cup diced tomatoes
- 2 cloves garlic, minced
- 1/4 cup olive oil
- 2 tablespoons tomato paste
- 1 teaspoon dried oregano
- 1 teaspoon dried basil
- Salt and pepper to taste
- Fresh basil leaves for garnish
- Cooked quinoa or couscous for serving

Directions:

1. In your crock pot, combine the fresh sardines, diced onions, diced bell

peppers, diced zucchini, diced tomatoes, minced garlic, olive oil, tomato paste, dried oregano, dried basil, salt, and pepper.
2. Stir to combine.
3. Cover and cook on LOW for 3 hours, or until the sardines are tender and cooked through.
4. Serve over cooked quinoa or couscous, garnished with fresh basil leaves.

Nutritional Value (Amount per Serving):

Calories: 291; Fat: 17.86; Carb: 11.82; Protein: 20.7

Crock Pot Shrimp and Mushroom Risotto

Prep Time: 15 Minutes Cook Time: 2 Hours 30 Minutes Serves: 4

Ingredients:

- 1 pound large shrimp, peeled and deveined
- 2 cups Arborio rice
- 1 cup sliced mushrooms
- 1 cup diced onions
- 2 cloves garlic, minced
- 4 cups chicken broth
- 1/2 cup dry white wine
- 1/2 cup grated Parmesan cheese
- 2 tablespoons butter
- Salt and pepper to taste
- Chopped fresh parsley for garnish

Directions:

1. In your crock pot, combine the shrimp, Arborio rice, sliced mushrooms, diced onions, minced garlic, chicken broth, dry white wine, grated Parmesan cheese, butter, salt, and pepper.
2. Stir to combine.
3. Cover and cook on LOW for 2.5 hours, or until the rice is tender and the shrimp are cooked through.
4. Serve hot, garnished with chopped fresh parsley.

Nutritional Value (Amount per Serving):

Calories: 746; Fat: 41.46; Carb: 40.85; Protein: 68.12

Mediterranean Crock Pot Mussels with Tomato Sauce

Prep Time: 20 Minutes Cook Time: 2 Hours Serves: 4

Ingredients:

- 2 pounds mussels, cleaned and debearded
- 2 cups diced tomatoes
- 1 cup diced onions
- 1 cup diced bell peppers (red and green)
- 2 cloves garlic, minced
- 1/4 cup olive oil
- 1/4 cup white wine
- 1 teaspoon dried oregano
- 1 teaspoon dried basil
- Salt and pepper to taste
- Fresh basil leaves for garnish
- Crusty bread for serving

Directions:

1. In your crock pot, combine the cleaned mussels, diced tomatoes, diced onions, diced bell peppers, minced garlic, olive oil, white wine, dried oregano, dried basil, salt, and pepper.
2. Stir to combine.
3. Cover and cook on LOW for 2 hours, or until the mussels have opened and are cooked.
4. Serve hot, garnished with fresh basil leaves, and provide crusty bread for soaking up the delicious tomato sauce.

Nutritional Value (Amount per Serving):

Calories: 372; Fat: 19.09; Carb: 20.58; Protein: 29.26

Crock Pot Cajun Catfish Gumbo

Prep Time: 20 Minutes Cook Time: 4 Hours Serves: 8

Ingredients:

- 2 pounds catfish fillets, cut into chunks
- 1 cup diced onions
- 1 cup diced bell peppers (red and green)
- 1 cup diced celery
- 2 cloves garlic, minced
- 1 can (14.5 ounces) diced tomatoes
- 4 cups chicken broth
- 1/4 cup all-purpose flour
- 1/4 cup vegetable oil
- 2 tablespoons Cajun seasoning
- Salt and pepper to taste
- Cooked rice for serving
- Chopped fresh parsley for garnish

Directions:

1. In your crock pot, combine the catfish chunks, diced onions, diced bell

peppers, diced celery, minced garlic, diced tomatoes, and chicken broth.
2. Stir to combine.
3. In a separate skillet, make a roux by heating the vegetable oil over medium heat and gradually adding the flour while stirring constantly. Cook until the roux is dark brown but not burned.
4. Add the roux to the crock pot mixture and stir well.
5. Season with Cajun seasoning, salt, and pepper.
6. Cover and cook on LOW for 4 hours.
7. Serve over cooked rice, garnished with chopped fresh parsley.

Nutritional Value (Amount per Serving):

Calories: 399; Fat: 18.58; Carb: 9.82; Protein: 45.93

Creamy Crock Pot Tuna and Spinach Pasta

Prep Time: 15 Minutes Cook Time: 2 Hours 30 Minutes Serves: 4

Ingredients:

- 12 ounces canned tuna, drained
- 2 cups fresh spinach leaves
- 2 cups cooked pasta
- 1 cup diced tomatoes
- 1/2 cup diced onions
- 2 cloves garlic, minced
- 1 cup shredded mozzarella cheese
- 1/4 cup grated Parmesan cheese
- 1 cup heavy cream
- 2 tablespoons butter
- Salt and pepper to taste
- Fresh basil leaves for garnish

Directions:

1. In your crock pot, combine the drained tuna, fresh spinach leaves, cooked pasta, diced tomatoes, diced onions, minced garlic, shredded mozzarella cheese, grated Parmesan cheese, heavy cream, butter, salt, and pepper.
2. Stir to combine.
3. Cover and cook on LOW for 2.5 hours, or until the pasta is heated through, and the cheese is melted and bubbly.

Nutritional Value (Amount per Serving):

Calories: 405; Fat: 20.1; Carb: 27.14; Protein: 31.02

Mediterranean Crock Pot Octopus Salad

Prep Time: 20 Minutes Cook Time: 2 Hours Serves: 4

Ingredients:

- 2 pounds octopus, cleaned and sliced into rings
- 1 cup diced tomatoes
- 1 cup diced cucumbers

- 1/2 cup diced red onions
- 1/4 cup chopped fresh parsley
- 2 cloves garlic, minced
- 1/4 cup olive oil
- 2 tablespoons red wine vinegar
- Salt and pepper to taste
- Lemon wedges for garnish

Directions:

1. In your crock pot, combine the octopus rings, diced tomatoes, diced cucumbers, diced red onions, chopped fresh parsley, minced garlic, olive oil, red wine vinegar, salt, and pepper.
2. Stir to combine.
3. Cover and cook on LOW for 2 hours, or until the octopus is tender.
4. Serve hot or chilled, garnished with lemon wedges.

Nutritional Value (Amount per Serving):

Calories: 333; Fat: 16.08; Carb: 11.07; Protein: 34.95

Crock Pot Tuna and White Bean Stew

Prep Time: 15 Minutes Cook Time: 3 Hours Serves: 6

Ingredients:

- 2 cans (5 ounces each) tuna, drained and flaked
- 2 cans (15 ounces each) white beans, drained and rinsed
- 1 cup diced tomatoes
- 1 cup diced onions
- 2 cloves garlic, minced
- 1/2 cup chicken broth
- 1/4 cup olive oil
- 1 teaspoon dried thyme
- Salt and pepper to taste
- Fresh parsley for garnish
- Crusty bread for serving

Directions:

1. In your crock pot, combine the flaked tuna, white beans, diced tomatoes, diced onions, minced garlic, chicken broth, olive oil, dried thyme, salt, and pepper.
2. Stir to combine.
3. Cover and cook on LOW for 3 hours.
4. Serve hot, garnished with fresh parsley, and provide crusty bread for dipping.

Nutritional Value (Amount per Serving):

Calories: 385; Fat: 11.66; Carb: 41.98; Protein: 29.9

Crock Pot Coconut Curry Mussels

Prep Time: 15 Minutes Cook Time: 2 Hours Serves: 4

Ingredients:

- 2 pounds mussels, cleaned and debearded
- 1 can (14 ounces) coconut milk
- 2 tablespoons red curry paste
- 1 cup diced tomatoes
- 1 cup diced onions
- 2 cloves garlic, minced
- 1 tablespoon fish sauce
- 1 tablespoon brown sugar
- 1 lime, juiced
- Fresh cilantro leaves for garnish
- Cooked rice or crusty bread for serving

Directions:

1. In your crock pot, combine the cleaned mussels, coconut milk, red curry paste, diced tomatoes, diced onions, minced garlic, fish sauce, and brown sugar.
2. Stir to combine.
3. Cover and cook on LOW for 2 hours, or until the mussels have opened and are cooked.
4. Stir in the lime juice.
5. Serve hot, garnished with fresh cilantro leaves, and provide cooked rice or crusty bread for soaking up the coconut curry sauce.

Nutritional Value (Amount per Serving):

Calories: 662; Fat: 36.07; Carb: 36.01; Protein: 50.86

Crock Pot Mediterranean Clam Linguine

Prep Time: 15 Minutes Cook Time: 3 Hours Serves: 4

Ingredients:

- 2 pounds little neck clams, cleaned
- 2 cups diced tomatoes
- 1 cup diced onions
- 1 cup diced bell peppers (red and green)
- 2 cloves garlic, minced
- 1/4 cup olive oil
- 1/4 cup white wine

- 1 teaspoon dried oregano
- 1 teaspoon dried basil
- Salt and pepper to taste
- Cooked linguine for serving
- Fresh basil leaves for garnish
- Grated Parmesan cheese for serving

Directions:

1. In your crock pot, combine the cleaned little neck clams, diced tomatoes, diced onions, diced bell peppers, minced garlic, olive oil, white wine, dried oregano, dried basil, salt, and pepper.
2. Stir to combine.
3. Cover and cook on LOW for 3 hours, or until the clams have opened and are cooked.
4. Serve over cooked linguine, garnished with fresh basil leaves and grated Parmesan cheese.

Nutritional Value (Amount per Serving):

Calories: 488; Fat: 22.02; Carb: 33.96; Protein: 40.24

Crock Pot Tuna Noodle Casserole

Prep Time: 25 Minutes Cook Time: 2 Hours Serves: 6

Ingredients:

- 14 ounces egg noodles
- 21 ounces canned cream of mushroom soup ((2 10.5 ounce cans))
- 2 cups shredded cheddar cheese (divided)
- 1 cup milk
- 14 ounces canned tuna ((2 7 ounce cans), drained)
- 10 ounces frozen peas
- 4 ounces Jarred diced pimentos (drained)
- 1 pinch Kosher salt
- 1 pinch freshly ground black pepper
- ¼ cup plain bread crumbs

Directions:

1. In a large pot on the stove-top, cook the egg noodles according to the directions on the package until just al dente. Drain.
2. In a large mixing bowl, combine together the cream of mushroom soup, 1 cup of the cheese, milk, tuna, peas, pimentos, salt and pepper until well mixed.
3. Add the cooked and drained noodles to the mixing bowl and toss.
4. Spray the inside of a casserole slow cooker with non-stick cooking spray

and add mixed ingredients.
5. Evenly sprinkle the casserole with the remaining 1 cup of cheese and breadcrumbs.
6. Cover and cook on HIGH for 2 hours or on LOW for 3 to 4 hours.
7. Serve and enjoy.

Nutritional Value (Amount per Serving):

Calories: 285; Fat: 8.41; Carb: 31.44; Protein: 21.63

Creamy Crock Pot Lobster Mac and Cheese

Prep Time: 20 Minutes Cook Time: 2 Hours 30 Minutes Serves: 6

Ingredients:

- 1 pound cooked lobster meat, chopped
- 12 ounces elbow macaroni, cooked and drained
- 2 cups shredded sharp cheddar cheese
- 1 cup shredded Gruyere cheese
- 1/2 cup grated Parmesan cheese
- 2 cups half-and-half
- 1/2 cup unsalted butter
- 2 tablespoons all-purpose flour
- 1 teaspoon dry mustard
- Salt and pepper to taste
- Fresh chives for garnish

Directions:

1. In your crock pot, combine the chopped lobster meat, cooked and drained elbow macaroni, shredded cheddar cheese, shredded Gruyere cheese, and grated Parmesan cheese.
2. In a saucepan, melt the butter over medium heat. Stir in the flour and dry mustard, cooking for a minute.
3. Gradually whisk in the half-and-half, stirring until the mixture thickens.
4. Pour the sauce over the macaroni and cheese mixture in the crock pot.
5. Stir to combine and season with salt and pepper.
6. Cover and cook on LOW for 2.5 hours, or until the mac and cheese is hot and bubbly.
7. Serve hot, garnished with fresh chives.

Nutritional Value (Amount per Serving):

Calories: 633; Fat: 26.01; Carb: 57.58; Protein: 45.82

Crock Pot Tortellini Shrimp Alfredo

Prep Time: 5 Minutes Cook Time: 2 Hours 30 Minutes Serves: 4

Ingredients:

- 16 ounces frozen peeled and deveined large shrimp (thawed)
- 22 ounces of jarred Alfredo sauce
- 16 ounce bag of frozen tortellini (do not thaw)
- 2 teaspoons Italian seasoning
- optional for serving: fresh basil and Parmesan cheese

Directions:

1. Spray the inside of the slow cooker with nonstick spray.
2. Add the jar of Alfredo sauce, frozen tortellini, and Italian seasoning to the slow cooker and stir to combine. Cook on high 2 to 2½ hours until the pasta is tender.
3. Add the thawed shrimp and continue cooking about 30 minutes to 1 hour longer until the shrimp are pink and no longer translucent. Stir in the remaining Alfredo sauce and warm if needed.
4. Adjust salt and pepper to taste. Serve and enjoy!

Nutritional Value (Amount per Serving):

Calories: 1131; Fat: 64.91; Carb: 107.26; Protein: 31.26

Crock Pot Teriyaki Salmon

Prep Time: 15 Minutes Cook Time: 2 Hours Serves: 4

Ingredients:

- 4 salmon fillets
- 1/2 cup teriyaki sauce
- 1/4 cup honey
- 2 cloves garlic, minced
- 1 teaspoon ginger paste or minced ginger
- 1/2 teaspoon red pepper flakes (adjust to taste)
- Sliced green onions for garnish
- Cooked rice for serving

Directions:

1. In your crock pot, place the salmon fillets.
2. In a bowl, whisk together the teriyaki sauce, honey, minced garlic, ginger paste, and red pepper flakes.
3. Pour the teriyaki mixture over the salmon.
4. Cover and cook on LOW for 2 hours, or until the salmon is flaky.

5. Serve over cooked rice, garnished with sliced green onions.

Nutritional Value (Amount per Serving):

Calories: 264; Fat: 7.59; Carb: 25.46; Protein: 23.13

Crock Pot Coconut-Lime Mahi Mahi

Prep Time: 15 Minutes Cook Time: 2 Hours 30 Minutes Serves: 4

Ingredients:

- 4 mahi mahi fillets
- 1 can (14 ounces) coconut milk
- Zest and juice of 2 limes
- 2 cloves garlic, minced
- 1 teaspoon dried thyme
- Salt and pepper to taste
- Fresh cilantro leaves for garnish
- Cooked quinoa or rice for serving

Directions:

1. In your crock pot, place the mahi mahi fillets.
2. In a bowl, combine the coconut milk, lime zest, lime juice, minced garlic, dried thyme, salt, and pepper.
3. Pour the coconut-lime mixture over the fish.
4. Cover and cook on LOW for 2.5 hours, or until the mahi mahi is cooked through.
5. Serve over cooked quinoa or rice, garnished with fresh cilantro leaves.

Nutritional Value (Amount per Serving):

Calories: 491; Fat: 39.08; Carb: 17.31; Protein: 22.27

Chapter 6: Pastas, Grains and Beans

Mediterranean Quinoa and Vegetable Pilaf

Prep Time: 20 Minutes Cook Time: 4 Hours Serves: 6-8

Ingredients:

- 1 cup quinoa, rinsed
- 2 cups vegetable broth
- 1 cup cherry tomatoes, halved
- 1 cup bell peppers (mixed colors), diced
- 1 cup artichoke hearts, quartered
- 1/2 cup kalamata olives, sliced
- 3 cloves garlic, minced
- 1 teaspoon dried basil
- 1 teaspoon dried oregano
- Salt and pepper to taste
- 2 tablespoons olive oil

Directions:

1. Combine quinoa, vegetable broth, cherry tomatoes, bell peppers, artichoke hearts, olives, minced garlic, dried basil, and dried oregano in the Crock Pot.
2. Season with salt and pepper. Drizzle olive oil over the ingredients.
3. Stir gently to mix everything together.
4. Cover and cook on low for 4 hours or until quinoa is tender.
5. Fluff the quinoa with a fork before serving. Adjust seasoning if needed.

Nutritional Value (Amount per Serving):

Calories: 157; Fat: 6.44; Carb: 21.45; Protein: 4.65

Crock Pot Greek Lemon Orzo with Spinach

Prep Time: 15 Minutes Cook Time: 3 Hours Serves: 4-6

Ingredients:

- 1 cup orzo pasta
- 4 cups vegetable broth
- 2 cups fresh spinach, chopped
- 1/2 cup feta cheese, crumbled
- 1/4 cup fresh dill, chopped
- 1 lemon, juiced and zested
- 2 tablespoons olive oil
- Salt and pepper to taste

Directions:

1. In the Crock Pot, combine orzo, vegetable broth, chopped spinach, feta cheese, fresh dill, lemon juice, lemon zest, and olive oil.
2. Season with salt and pepper. Stir well.
3. Cover and cook on low for 3 hours or until the orzo is cooked al dente.
4. Before serving, fluff the orzo and adjust seasoning if necessary.

Nutritional Value (Amount per Serving):

Calories: 141; Fat: 8.89; Carb: 12.81; Protein: 3.44

Slow-Cooked Mediterranean Pasta Puttanesca

Prep Time: 15 Minutes   Cook Time: 4 Hours   Serves: 4-6

Ingredients:

- 1 pound penne pasta, cooked al dente
- 1 can (14 oz) diced tomatoes
- 1/2 cup Kalamata olives, sliced
- 1/4 cup capers
- 3 cloves garlic, minced
- 1 teaspoon red pepper flakes
- 2 tablespoons olive oil
- 1/4 cup fresh basil, chopped
- Salt and pepper to taste
- Grated Parmesan cheese for serving

Directions:

1. In the Crock Pot, combine cooked penne pasta, diced tomatoes, sliced Kalamata olives, capers, minced garlic, red pepper flakes, olive oil, and chopped fresh basil.
2. Season with salt and pepper. Stir well.
3. Cover and cook on low for 4 hours, allowing flavors to meld.
4. Before serving, sprinkle with grated Parmesan cheese. Adjust seasoning if necessary.

Nutritional Value (Amount per Serving):

Calories: 198; Fat: 7.71; Carb: 30.29; Protein: 3.75

Crock Pot Mediterranean Pasta e Fagioli

Prep Time: 15 Minutes   Cook Time: 5 Hours   Serves: 6-8

Ingredients:

- 1 cup ditalini pasta, uncooked
- 2 cans (15 oz each) cannellini beans, drained and rinsed
- 1 can (14 oz) diced tomatoes
- 1 cup celery, diced
- 1 cup carrots, diced
- 1 large onion, finely chopped
- 3 cloves garlic, minced
- 4 cups vegetable broth
- 1 teaspoon dried basil
- 1 teaspoon dried oregano
- Salt and pepper to taste
- 2 tablespoons olive oil
- Grated Parmesan cheese for serving

Directions:

1. In the Crock Pot, combine ditalini pasta, cannellini beans, diced tomatoes, diced celery, diced carrots, chopped onion, minced garlic, vegetable broth, dried basil, and dried oregano.
2. Season with salt and pepper. Drizzle olive oil over the ingredients. Stir well.

3. Cover and cook on low for 5 hours or until the pasta and vegetables are tender.
4. Before serving, sprinkle with grated Parmesan cheese. Adjust seasoning if necessary.

Nutritional Value (Amount per Serving):

Calories: 195; Fat: 6.02; Carb: 30.19; Protein: 6.85

Slow Cooker Red Lentil Curry

Prep Time: 7 Minutes Cook Time: 3 Hours Serves: 6

Ingredients:

- 2 red onions diced
- 400 g red lentils (2 cups) uncooked
- 2 cloves garlic minced
- 950 ml water (4 cups)
- 800 g chopped tomatoes (2 400g tins)
- 3 teaspoon ground coriander
- 3 teaspoon ground ginger
- 2 teaspoon garam masala
- 2 teaspoon ground cumin
- 1/4 teaspoon ground cinnamon
- 1/2 teaspoon ground turmeric
- 1 teaspoon mild chili powder
- 1 teaspoon paprika
- 2 vegetable stock cubes or vegan based
- Seasoning (salt and pepper to taste)

Directions:

1. Chuck everything in to your slow cooker, place the lid on top and cook on low for 6-7 hours or on high for 3-4 hours.
2. If desired, stir in half a can of coconut milk or cream.
3. Serve with boiled rice or over a baked potato and top with fresh coriander leaves.

Nutritional Value (Amount per Serving):

Calories: 329; Fat: 6.64; Carb: 52.52; Protein: 18.49

Vegan Black Bean and Quinoa Stuffed Bell Peppers

Prep Time: 20 Minutes Cook Time: 4 Hours Serves: 4

Ingredients:

- 4 bell peppers, tops removed and seeds removed
- 1 cup quinoa, rinsed
- 2 cups vegetable broth
- 2 cans (15 oz each) black beans, drained and rinsed
- 1 can (14 oz) diced tomatoes

- 1 teaspoon chili powder
- Salt and pepper to taste
- Sliced avocado for garnish

Directions:

1. Stuff each bell pepper with quinoa, black beans, diced tomatoes, chili powder, salt, and pepper.
2. Place the stuffed peppers in the crock pot.
3. Cover and cook on low for 4 hours or until the peppers are tender.
4. Garnish with sliced avocado before serving.

Nutritional Value (Amount per Serving):

Calories: 555; Fat: 11.42; Carb: 90.78; Protein: 27.44

Slow-Cooked Vegan Moroccan Chickpea Stew

Prep Time: 10 Minutes Cook Time: 3 Hours Serves: 6

Ingredients:

- 1 tablespoon olive oil
- 1 small white onion diced
- 2 garlic cloves minced
- 1 tablespoon minced fresh ginger
- 1 teaspoon cumin
- 1 teaspoon paprika
- 1/4 teaspoon coriander
- 1/4 teaspoon cinnamon
- 1/4 teaspoon ginger
- 1 teaspoon kosher salt
- 1/2 teaspoon black pepper
- 1-14.5 ounce can chickpeas drained and rinsed
- 1-14.5 ounce can diced fire-roasted tomatoes
- 1 medium sweet potato diced
- 2 carrots trimmed and diced
- 1 red pepper diced
- 1 cup green lentils
- 2 tablespoons harissa paste
- 4 cups low sodium vegetable broth
- Chopped parsley for serving

Directions:

1. In a skillet or stove-top safe slow cooker pot, heat the olive oil over medium heat. Sauté the onions until they are soft and translucent, about 5-7 minutes. Add the minced garlic, minced fresh ginger, dried spices (cumin, paprika, coriander, cinnamon & ginger), salt and pepper. Cook until fragrant, about 1 minute.
2. Transfer the onions to the slow cooker. Add the chickpeas, tomatoes, sweet potatoes, carrots, red peppers, lentils, harissa and vegetable broth.
3. Cook on high for 3-4 hours or on low for 6-7 hours until the vegetables and lentils are tender.
4. Divide into bowls and garnish with chopped parsley before serving.

Nutritional Value (Amount per Serving):

Calories: 183; Fat: 4.98; Carb: 31.11; Protein: 7.18

Slow Cooker Vegan Barley and Mushroom Risotto

Prep Time: 10 Minutes Cook Time: 3 Hours 10 Minutes Serves: 4

Ingredients:

- 2 tablespoons extra-virgin olive oil
- 1 large onion, finely chopped
- Kosher salt and freshly ground black pepper
- 1 pound cremini mushrooms, sliced
- 1 1/2 cups pearl barley
- 4 sprigs fresh thyme
- 8 ounces carrots, finely chopped
- 3 cups lower-sodium vegetable broth
- 1 ounce Parmesan, grated (2/3 cup)
- 1 tablespoon sherry vinegar
- 1/4 cup chopped fresh flat-leaf parsley

Directions:

1. Heat the olive oil in a large skillet over medium-high heat. Add the onions and 1/8 teaspoon each salt and pepper and cook, stirring occasionally, until lightly browned, about 5 minutes. Add the mushrooms and cook, stirring occasionally, until browned, about 2 minutes. Stir in the barley and thyme and cook, stirring, until the barley is just golden, about 2 minutes.
2. Transfer to a slow cooker and add the carrots, broth, 1 1/2 cups water and 1/4 teaspoon salt. Cover and cook on high until the liquid is absorbed and the carrots and barley are tender, about 3 hours.
3. Discard the thyme and stir in the Parmesan, vinegar, 1/2 teaspoon salt and 1/4 teaspoon pepper. Thin out the risotto with warm water for desired consistency as needed. Top with parsley and season to taste with salt and pepper.

Nutritional Value (Amount per Serving):

Calories: 706; Fat: 6.33; Carb: 156.2; Protein: 23.19

Slow Cooker Sweet Potato Black Bean Chili

Prep Time: 20 Minutes Cook Time: 4 Hours Serves: 6

Ingredients:

- 2 medium sweet potatoes, peeled and cubed
- 1 medium yellow onion, finely chopped

- 1 poblano pepper, seeds removed, finely chopped
- 4 garlic cloves, minced
- 2 (15-oz.) cans black beans, rinsed and drained
- 1 (15-oz.) can dark red kidney beans, rinsed and drained
- 2 (14.5-oz.) cans fire-roasted diced tomatoes with green chilies
- 1 cup vegetable broth (sub beef or bone broth if not making vegetarian)
- 2 Tbsp. tomato paste
- 2 Tbsp. chili powder
- 1 Tbsp. ground cumin
- 2 tsp. smoked paprika
- 1 tsp. dried oregano
- 2 tsp. kosher salt

Directions:

1. Grease a slow cooker with non-stick cooking spray. Combine all chili ingredients; stir well to combine.
2. Cook on LOW for 8 hours, or on HIGH for 4 hours, until the sweet potatoes are tender. Serve with your favorite toppings.

Nutritional Value (Amount per Serving):

Calories: 392; Fat: 3.71; Carb: 72.13; Protein: 21.46

Vegan Mushroom Barley Soup

Prep Time: 15 Minutes Cook Time: Hours Serves: 8

Ingredients:

- 8 oz baby bella mushrooms, sliced
- 5 oz shiitake mushrooms, sliced
- 8 oz white mushrooms, sliced
- 1 large carrot diced
- 1 large celery stalk, diced
- 1 small onion, diced
- 1 tablespoon minced garlic
- 1 tablespoon Worcestershire sauce
- 1 tablespoon soy sauce I use reduced sodium
- 1 teaspoon dried basil
- 1 teaspoon dried thyme
- ¾ cup pearl barley
- 8 cups broth vegetable, mushroom or beef broth would all work well

Directions:

1. Place slow cooker liner into slow cooker, if using
2. Place mushrooms into slow cooker

3. Add diced vegetables to slow cooker
4. Add garlic, Worcestershire sauce, say sauce, basil, thyme and barley to slow cooker.
5. Pour broth over ingredients in slow cooker
6. Stir, cover and cook on low for 6 hours.
7. Serve in bowls and enjoy.

Nutritional Value (Amount per Serving):

Calories: 321; Fat: 7.63; Carb: 57.74; Protein: 11.58

Crock Pot Vegan Black Bean and Brown Rice Salad

Prep Time: 1 Minutes Cook Time: 2 Hours Serves: 4

Ingredients:

- 1 cup brown rice
- 2 cups vegetable broth
- 2 cans (15 oz each) black beans, drained and rinsed
- 1 bell pepper, diced
- 1/2 cup red onion, finely chopped
- 1/4 cup fresh cilantro, chopped
- Zest and juice of 2 limes
- Salt and pepper to taste

Directions:

1. In the crock pot, combine brown rice, vegetable broth, black beans, diced bell pepper, finely chopped red onion, chopped fresh cilantro, lime zest, lime juice, salt, and pepper.
2. Stir well, cover, and cook on low for 2 hours or until the rice is cooked.
3. Fluff with a fork before serving this zesty black bean and brown rice salad.

Nutritional Value (Amount per Serving):

Calories: 550; Fat: 2.99; Carb: 108.6; Protein: 24.73

Crock Pot Bacon Ranch Chicken Pasta

Prep Time: 10 Minutes Cook Time: 6 Hours Serves: 8

Ingredients:

- 3 boneless skinless chicken breasts
- 12 strips bacon (cooked and crumbled)
- 1 tsp minced garlic
- 1 packet dry ranch dressing mix (1 oz packet)

- 1 cup chicken broth
- 2 cups heavy whipping cream
- 16 oz. rotini pasta (cooked to al dente)
- 2 cups cheddar cheese (shredded)

Directions:

1. Place the chicken, bacon, garlic, ranch mix and chicken broth in a crock pot.
2. Cover and cook on low for 6-8 hours or on high for 3-4 hours.
3. Shred the chicken and return back to the crock pot.
4. Then stir in the heavy whipping cream, pasta and cheddar cheese. Cover and let sit for a few minutes to allow the cheese to melt.
5. Serve immediately while warm and enjoy!

Nutritional Value (Amount per Serving):

Calories: 713; Fat: 46.78; Carb: 19.52; Protein: 52.43

Creamy Sun Dried Tomato Chicken Pasta

Prep Time: 10 Minutes Cook Time: 6 Hours Serves: 6

Ingredients:

- 4 boneless skinless chicken breasts
- 2 cups chicken broth
- 1 teaspoon salt
- 1 teaspoon pepper
- 2 Tablespoons basil dried
- 1/2 cup sun dried tomatoes in olive oil
- 2 cups heavy cream
- 16 oz angel hair pasta cooked
- 1/2 cup grated parmesan cheese

Directions:

1. Place the chicken in the slow cooker.
2. Pour chicken stock on top.
3. Season with salt, pepper, and basil.
4. Pour sun dried tomatoes on top.
5. Cook on low 6-8 hours or until chicken is tender.
6. 5 minutes before serving, stir in the heavy cream.
7. After it is combined, stir in the grated parmesan cheese and the angel hair pasta.
8. Serve immediately.

Nutritional Value (Amount per Serving):

Calories: 635; Fat: 29.27; Carb: 26.86; Protein: 63.91

Crock Pot Rice and Bean Bowl

Prep Time: 15 Minutes Cook Time: 2 Hours Serves: 4

Ingredients:

- 1 small onion, chopped
- 2 tsp. minced garlic
- 2 15 oz. cans black beans, rinsed well and drained
- 1 cup uncooked brown rice
- 2 4 oz. cans diced green chilies
- 1 14 oz. can vegetable broth
- 1/2 tsp. ground cumin
- 1 tsp. Mexican oregano
- 2 tsp. Sazon seasoning (optional, but it adds a lot of flavor)
- 6 pieces Mozzarella string cheese
- 1 cup green onions, sliced (more or less to taste)

Directions:

1. Spray the inside of a slow cooker with non-stick spray.
2. Chop up the onion.
3. If using canned beans, rinse in a colander placed in the sink (until no more foam appears) and let the beans drain.
4. Put diced onion, minced garlic, black beans, rice, vegetable broth, diced green chilies, ground cumin, Mexican oregano, and Sazon (if using) into the slow cooker.
5. Cook on high for 1 hour 30 minutes.
6. Cut 6 sticks Mozzarella string cheese into slices (or cut 6 oz. cheese into cubes if not using string cheese.)
7. Gently stir the cheese into the rice and bean mixture and cook 20-30 more minutes, or until the rice is done and the cheese is melting.
8. Chop up desired amount of green onions.
9. Turn off heat, stir in the green onions, and serve hot with salsa, diced avocado, and/or sour cream to add at the table.

Nutritional Value (Amount per Serving):

Calories: 1197; Fat: 17.32; Carb: 202.21; Protein: 62.5

Slow-Cooked Vegan Quinoa and Corn Casserole

Prep Time: 20 Minutes Cook Time: 3 Hours Serves: 4

Ingredients:

- 1 cup quinoa, rinsed
- 2 cups vegetable broth
- 1 cup corn kernels (fresh or frozen)
- 1 bell pepper, diced
- 1 onion, diced
- 2 cloves garlic, minced
- 1/2 cup vegan cheese, shredded
- 1/4 cup vegan sour cream
- Salt and pepper to taste
- Chopped fresh chives for garnish

Directions:

1. In the crock pot, combine quinoa, vegetable broth, corn kernels, diced bell pepper, diced onion, minced garlic, vegan cheese, vegan sour cream, salt, and pepper.
2. Stir well, cover, and cook on low for 3 hours.
3. Garnish with chopped fresh chives before serving as a creamy quinoa and corn casserole.

Nutritional Value (Amount per Serving):

Calories: 285; Fat: 8.88; Carb: 41.61; Protein: 11.57

Slow Cooker Vegan Black Eyed Peas

Prep Time: 15 Minutes Cook Time: 7 Hours Serves: 5

Ingredients:

- 2 cups black-eyed peas, dry, uncooked, soaked overnight
- 4 cups water
- 1 tbsp olive oil, extra virgin
- 1 tsp cumin seeds
- 2 bay leaves
- 1 black cardamon, seeds, crushed
- 3 tsp garlic, fresh, crushed
- 1 onion, large, chopped
- 2 tsp curry powder
- 1 tsp paprika
- 2 tsp coriander powder, made from grinding whole coriander seeds
- ½ tsp red chili
- 1½ tsp salt
- 1 cup tomato puree, thick consistency,
- 1 cup cilantro, fresh, washed, chopped
- 1 lemon, fresh, juice

Directions:

1. Rinse and drain the soaked black-eyed peas thoroughly. Place the black-eyed peas, water, and bay leaves in a slow cooker. Set it to high heat.
2. In a medium pan, heat olive oil over medium heat. Add cumin seeds, bay leaves and crushed cardamom seeds. Fry until fragrant, being careful not to burn them.
3. Add crushed garlic and onion and sauté until the onions turn golden brown.
4. Stir in curry powder, coriander powder, paprika, and red chili. Sizzle for a few seconds.

5. Add the tomato puree and cook for an additional minute, mixing well.
6. Transfer the tomato-spice mixture into the slow cooker with the black-eyed peas. Stir thoroughly.
7. Cover the slow cooker and cook on high for 7 hours. Once cooked, garnish with fresh cilantro and lemon juice.

Nutritional Value (Amount per Serving):

Calories: 225; Fat: 3.89; Carb: 49.68; Protein: 4.22

Crock Pot Ginger Soy Green Beans

Prep Time: 10 Minutes Cook Time: 2 Hours Serves: 4

Ingredients:

- 1 pound of fresh green beans, trimmed
- 2 tablespoons of soy sauce
- 1 tablespoon of honey
- 2 cloves of garlic, minced
- 1 teaspoon of ginger, minced
- 2 tablespoons of sesame oil
- Salt and black pepper to taste
- Toasted sesame seeds for garnish (optional)

Directions:

1. Place the trimmed green beans in the crock pot.
2. In a bowl, whisk together the soy sauce, honey, minced garlic, minced ginger, sesame oil, salt, and black pepper.
3. Drizzle the ginger soy mixture over the green beans and toss to coat.
4. Cover and cook on low for 2 hours or until the green beans are tender and the sauce has reduced and coated the beans.
5. Garnish with toasted sesame seeds before serving, if desired.

Nutritional Value (Amount per Serving):

Calories: 143; Fat: 9.76; Carb: 13.38; Protein: 2.52

Slow Cooker Spicy Black Beans

Prep Time: 10 Minutes Cook Time: 8 Hours Serves: 6

Ingredients:

- 3 cups dried black beans + water
- 4 cups chicken broth
- ½ cup chopped onion
- ½ cup chopped green pepper
- 1 can Rotel tomatoes
- 1 teaspoon cumin

- 1 teaspoon chili powder
- 1 teaspoon salt

Directions:

1. Rinse beans and soak overnight in water (3xs the volume of the beans).
2. Drain beans in the morning.
3. Add to a crock pot with chicken broth, onion, pepper, tomatoes, cumin, chili powder, and salt.
4. Cover and cook on low for 8 hours.

Nutritional Value (Amount per Serving):

Calories: 323; Fat: 12.12; Carb: 13.48; Protein: 38.12

Vegan Wild Rice and White Bean Casserole

Prep Time: 20 Minutes Cook Time: 4 Hours Serves: 4

Ingredients:

- 1 cup wild rice
- 4 cups vegetable broth
- 2 cans (15 oz each) white beans, drained and rinsed
- 1 cup spinach, chopped
- 1 onion, diced
- 2 cloves garlic, minced
- 1/4 cup vegan cheese, shredded
- Salt and pepper to taste
- Chopped fresh parsley for garnish

Directions:

1. In the crock pot, combine wild rice, vegetable broth, white beans, chopped spinach, diced onion, minced garlic, vegan cheese, salt, and pepper.
2. Stir well, cover, and cook on low for 4 hours.
3. Garnish with chopped fresh parsley before serving this creamy wild rice and white bean casserole.

Nutritional Value (Amount per Serving):

Calories: 498; Fat: 3.2; Carb: 91.89; Protein: 29.24

Chapter 7: Desserts

Greek Yogurt Berry Parfait

Prep Time: 15 Minutes Cook Time: 2 Hours Serves: 6

Ingredients:

- 2 cups Greek yogurt
- 1 cup mixed berries (strawberries, blueberries, raspberries)
- 1/4 cup honey
- 1 teaspoon vanilla extract
- 1/2 cup granola

Directions:

1. In a bowl, mix Greek yogurt, honey, and vanilla extract until well combined.
2. Layer the bottom of the crock pot with half of the yogurt mixture.
3. Add half of the mixed berries on top of the yogurt layer.
4. Sprinkle half of the granola evenly over the berries.
5. Repeat the layers with the remaining ingredients.
6. Cover the crock pot and cook on low for 2 hours.
7. Once done, let it cool for 10 minutes before serving.

Nutritional Value (Amount per Serving):

Calories: 157; Fat: 5.03; Carb: 24.06; Protein: 4.67

Orange and Almond Rice Pudding

Prep Time: 25 Minutes Cook Time: 3 Hours Serves: 8

Ingredients:

- 1 cup arborio rice
- 4 cups almond milk
- 1 cup sugar
- Zest of 2 oranges
- 1/2 cup sliced almonds

Directions:

1. Rinse the arborio rice under cold water and drain.
2. In the crock pot, combine rice, almond milk, sugar, and orange zest. Stir well.
3. Cover and cook on low for 3 hours, stirring occasionally.
4. In the last 30 minutes, stir in the sliced almonds.
5. Once the rice is creamy and cooked through, turn off the crock pot.
6. Allow it to cool slightly before serving.
7. Serve warm or chilled.

Nutritional Value (Amount per Serving):

Calories: 162; Fat: 4.63; Carb: 32.52; Protein: 2.83

Almond and Orange Blossom Cake

Prep Time: 25 Minutes   Cook Time: 2 Hours 30 Minutes   Serves: 12

Ingredients:

- 2 cups almond flour
- 1 cup sugar
- 1 teaspoon baking powder
- 1/2 teaspoon salt
- Zest of 2 oranges
- 4 eggs
- 1/2 cup olive oil
- 1/4 cup orange blossom water

Directions:

1. In a bowl, combine almond flour, sugar, baking powder, salt, and orange zest.
2. In another bowl, whisk together eggs, olive oil, and orange blossom water.
3. Combine wet and dry ingredients, mixing until well incorporated.
4. Grease the crock pot and pour in the batter.
5. Cover and cook on low for 2.5 hours or until a toothpick comes out clean.
6. Allow the cake to cool before slicing and serving.

Nutritional Value (Amount per Serving):

Calories: 164; Fat: 12.33; Carb: 10.64; Protein: 3.14

Pistachio and Honey Baklava Bites

Prep Time: 30 Minutes   Cook Time: 2 Hours   Serves: 15

Ingredients:

- 1 cup chopped pistachios
- 1/2 cup honey
- 1/2 cup unsalted butter, melted
- 1 package phyllo dough, thawed
- Ground cinnamon for dusting

Directions:

1. In a bowl, mix chopped pistachios with honey until well coated.
2. Brush melted butter on the bottom of the crock pot.
3. Place a layer of phyllo dough, brush with butter, and repeat for 4 layers.
4. Spread a third of the pistachio-honey mixture over the phyllo layers.
5. Repeat the layering process, ending with a layer of phyllo on top.
6. Before cooking, cut into bite-sized squares with a sharp knife.
7. Cover and cook on low for 2 hours or until golden brown.
8. Dust with ground cinnamon before serving.

Nutritional Value (Amount per Serving):

Calories: 123; Fat: 7.92; Carb: 12.65; Protein: 2.05

Lemon Lavender Panna Cotta

Prep Time: 20 Minutes Cook Time: 3 Hours Serves: 6

Ingredients:

- 2 cups heavy cream
- 1/2 cup sugar
- Zest of 2 lemons
- 1 tablespoon culinary lavender
- 1/4 cup cold water
- 2 1/2 teaspoons gelatin
- Fresh berries for garnish

Directions:

1. In a saucepan, heat the heavy cream and sugar over medium heat until it just begins to simmer. Remove from heat.
2. Add lemon zest and culinary lavender to the cream mixture. Let it steep for 10 minutes, then strain out the zest and lavender.
3. In a small bowl, sprinkle gelatin over cold water. Allow it to bloom for 5 minutes.
4. Add the bloomed gelatin to the warm cream mixture, stirring until fully dissolved.
5. Pour the mixture into the crock pot and cover. Cook on low for 3 hours.
6. After 3 hours, carefully transfer the panna cotta mixture into individual serving glasses or ramekins. Refrigerate for at least 2 hours or until set.
7. Garnish with fresh berries just before serving.

Nutritional Value (Amount per Serving):

Calories: 186; Fat: 15.17; Carb: 10.89; Protein: 2.73

Chocolate Peanut Clusters

Prep Time: 5 Minutes Cook Time: 2 Hours Serves: 20

Ingredients:

- 2 lbs white melting chocolate (white almond bark or candy coating)
- 4 oz sweet baking chocolate
- 2 cups semi sweet chocolate chips
- 16 oz salted dry roasted peanuts
- 8 oz unsalted dry roasted peanuts
- 8 oz cocktail peanuts

Directions:

1. Line your kitchen counter with parchment, or 3 baking sheets with parchment.
2. In a large slow cooker, add the white melting chocolate, sweet baking chocolate, and semi-sweet chocolate chips. Put the lid on and set to LOW

for 1-2 hours, stirring occasionally (you will want to check it to make sure it is not burning).
3. When the chocolates are all soft and melted enough, stir to combine them.
4. Add all of the nuts to the crock pot and stir them in well. Put the lid on and switch to Warm, or turn off the slow cooker (but leave the crock in the housing to stay warm).
5. Use an ice cream scoop or a Tablespoon, depending on how large you want your peanut clusters, to scoop small mounds onto the parchment paper. After you have used all of the mixture, rinse your crock with hot water.
6. The candies will take about an hour to really set. When they are set, transfer to an air tight container. These keep well for a week or so, and are wonderful to give as gifts.

Nutritional Value (Amount per Serving):

Calories: 572; Fat: 41.88; Carb: 41.64; Protein: 16.41

Crock Pot Chocolate Cherry Brownies

Prep Time: 5 Minutes Cook Time: 3 Hours Serves: 8

Ingredients:

- 1 box Brownie mix (unprepared, just the mix)
- 2 cans Cherry pie filling (mine were 21 ounces each)
- 2 sticks butter (unsalted) (2 sticks equals to 1 cup of butter)

Directions:

1. Spray your crock pot with non-stick spray. Add the cherry filling to your crock pot.
2. Melt your butter, and then mix it with the brownie mix in a large bowl.
3. Add the brownie mix and butter mixture on top of the cherries, and cook on high for about 3 hours.
4. Serve with ice cream or whipped cream on top.

Nutritional Value (Amount per Serving):

Calories: 170; Fat: 0.1; Carb: 41.44; Protein: 0.55

Slow Cooker Banana Split Cake

Prep Time: 15 Minutes Cook Time: 2 Hours Serves: 8

Ingredients:

- 1 box Yellow Cake Mix
- 1 cup vanilla ice cream, melted

- 1/4 cup water
- 1/2 cup vegetable oil
- 3 eggs
- 1 box (4-serving size) banana cream instant pudding and pie filling mix
- 24 large maraschino cherries
- 1/2 cup pecan pieces
- 1/2 gallon vanilla ice cream
- 1 cup hot fudge

Directions:

1. Spray a slow cooker with baking spray with flour.
2. In large bowl, stir together cake mix, melted ice cream, water, oil, eggs and pudding mix. Cut 12 of the maraschino cherries in half, and fold into batter along with 1/4 cup of the pecan pieces. Pour batter into a slow cooker. Top with remaining pecans and 8 more maraschino cherry halves.
3. Cover and cook on High heat setting 2 to 3 hours or until cake is set in center. To serve, spoon hot cake from slow cooker, and top with scoops of ice cream. Drizzle with hot fudge; top with remaining cherries.

Nutritional Value (Amount per Serving):

Calories: 529; Fat: 25.88; Carb: 68.95; Protein: 7.76

Slow Cooker Coconut Rice Pudding

Prep Time: 5 Minutes Cook Time: 3 Hours Serves: 8

Ingredients:

- 3 tablespoons salted butter (or margarine) divided use
- 6 cups milk 2% or higher
- 15 ounce can cream of coconut (not coconut water or coconut milk)
- 2 cups instant rice, uncooked (Minute Rice)
- ¼ teaspoon salt
- ½ teaspoon ground cinnamon
- ½ teaspoon vanilla extract
- toasted coconut for topping (optional)

Directions:

1. Butter a slow cooker. Make sure to rub the entire interior with the butter (or margarine.)
2. Pour milk and cream of coconut into the bottom of the slow cooker. Then pour in rice, salt, ground cinnamon and vanilla extract and stir well.
3. Top mixture with remaining butter (that you used to grease the crock pot.)
4. Cover slow cooker and cook for about 3-4 hours on low. Make sure to stir occasionally. This will help the rice soak up all of those delicious flavors as

it cooks.
5. Top with additional cinnamon before serving.
6. If you'd like, you can top individual servings with toasted coconut flakes. Place sweetened flaked coconut on a nonstick baking sheet. Place in a preheated 350F degree oven for about 10 minutes (making sure to rotate the pan every couple of minutes), until lightly golden brown.

Nutritional Value (Amount per Serving):

Calories: 389; Fat: 25.2; Carb: 32.99; Protein: 10.05

Crock Pot Gingerbread Pudding Cake

Prep Time: 20 Minutes Cook Time: 2 Hours 50 Minutes Serves: 6

Ingredients:

- 1/4 cup butter softened
- 1/4 cup granulated sugar
- 1 large egg
- 1 teaspoon vanilla
- 1/2 cup molasses
- 1 cup water
- 1 1/4 cups whole wheat flour or sub all purpose
- 3/4 teaspoon baking soda
- 1/2 teaspoon ground cinnamon
- 1/2 teaspoon ground ginger
- 1/4 teaspoon salt
- 1/8 teaspoon ground nutmeg
- 6 tablespoons brown sugar
- 3/4 cup hot water
- 1/4 cup butter melted

Directions:

1. With an electric mixer, beat butter and sugar until combined. Add egg and beat until combined. Add vanilla, molasses and water and beat (start on low!) until combined. There might be a few flecks of butter unincorporated, but that's okay.
2. Add the flour, baking soda, cinnamon, ginger, salt and nutmeg and beat until combined. Pour into a greased slow cooker.
3. Sprinkle batter with brown sugar. Combine hot water and melted butter and pour over brown sugar (no stirring!).
4. Cover with the lid and cook on high for 2.5-3 hours. Serve warm with ice cream or whipped cream.

Nutritional Value (Amount per Serving):

Calories: 455; Fat: 16.42; Carb: 74.96; Protein: 3.36

Slow Cooker Eggnog Rice Pudding

Prep Time: 5 Minutes Cook Time: 6 Hours Serves: 8

Ingredients:

- 12 cups eggnog
- 4 cups instant white rice uncooked
- Milk if you prefer your pudding chilled, optional
- ground cinnamon
- ground nutmeg
- dried cranberries
- rum

Directions:

1. Add eggnog and rice to slow cooker and mix well.
2. Cook on low, approximately 4 hours, giving it a quick stir about once every hour.
3. While pudding is cooking, pour yourself a glass of rum. Okay, now pour another glass and drop in some dried cranberries. Store in the fridge until ready to serve.
4. Serve warm or cold, garnished with a sprinkle of nutmeg, a dash of cinnamon, and some rum soaked cranberries.

Nutritional Value (Amount per Serving):

Calories: 571; Fat: 17.8; Carb: 77.53; Protein: 22.35

Peanut Butter Cup Cheesecake

Prep Time: 15 Minutes Cook Time: 2 Hours 30 Minutes Serves: 8

Ingredients:

- 1 1/2 cups chocolate cookie crumbs
- 1/4 cup unsalted butter, melted
- 16 oz cream cheese, softened
- 1 cup creamy peanut butter
- 1 cup granulated sugar
- 2 large eggs
- 1 tsp vanilla extract
- 1 cup semisweet chocolate chips
- 1/4 cup heavy cream
- Mini peanut butter cups for garnish (optional)

Directions:

1. Grease the inside of the crock pot.
2. In a mixing bowl, combine chocolate cookie crumbs and melted butter.
3. Press the mixture into the bottom of the crock pot to form the crust.
4. In another bowl, beat cream cheese, creamy peanut butter, granulated

sugar, eggs, and vanilla extract until smooth.
5. Pour the cream cheese mixture over the crust in the crock pot.
6. Cover and cook on low for 2 hours and 30 minutes, or until the cheesecake is set around the edges but slightly jiggly in the center.
7. Turn off the crock pot and let the cheesecake cool inside with the lid partially open.
8. In a microwave-safe bowl, melt the semisweet chocolate chips with heavy cream, stirring until smooth.
9. Pour the chocolate ganache over the cheesecake and spread it evenly.
10. Refrigerate the cheesecake for a few hours or until the ganache has set.
11. Serve chilled, optionally garnished with mini peanut butter cups.

Nutritional Value (Amount per Serving):

Calories: 921; Fat: 59.29; Carb: 83.49; Protein: 24.25

Slow Cooker Apricot Cobbler

Prep Time: 15 Minutes Cook Time: 3 Hours Serves: 6

Ingredients:

- 4 cups fresh or canned apricots, sliced
- 1 cup granulated sugar
- 1 cup all-purpose flour
- 2 tsp baking powder
- 1/4 tsp salt
- 1 cup milk
- 1/2 cup unsalted butter, melted
- Vanilla ice cream for serving (optional)

Directions:

1. Grease the inside of the crock pot.
2. Spread the sliced apricots evenly in the crock pot.
3. In a mixing bowl, whisk together granulated sugar, flour, baking powder, and salt.
4. Stir in milk and melted butter until a batter forms.
5. Pour the batter evenly over the apricots in the crock pot.
6. Cover and cook on low for 3 hours, or until the cobbler is set and the top is golden brown.
7. Serve warm, optionally with a scoop of vanilla ice cream.

Nutritional Value (Amount per Serving):

Calories: 491; Fat: 12.62; Carb: 94.16; Protein: 7.49

Butterscotch Pudding

Prep Time: 15 Minutes Cook Time: 2 Hours 50 Minutes Serves: 6

Ingredients:

- 125g unsalted butter, plus extra to grease
- 175g self-rising flour
- 50g dark brown soft sugar
- 1 large egg
- 150ml milk
- Finely grated zest of ½ lemon
- 1tsp vanilla extract
- 2tbsp golden syrup
- Icing sugar, to dust
- 1tbsp cornflour
- 100g dark brown soft sugar
- 150ml double cream
- 1tsp vanilla extract
- 2tbsp golden syrup

Directions:

1. Grease the pot of a slow cooker.
2. To make the cake, melt the butter in a small pan and set aside. Sift the flour into a large bowl and stir in the 50g dark brown soft sugar. To the butter, add the egg, milk, lemon zest, vanilla and the golden syrup and mix. Add wet ingredients to the flour bowl, and whisk until combined and smooth. Scrape mixture into the prepared cooking pot.
3. For the topping (which turns into the sauce) mix together the cornflour and muscovado sugar, and scatter mixture over the raw cake.
4. Next heat the cream, vanilla and syrup with 100ml water until just boiling. Take off the heat and immediately and carefully pour all over the cake. Cover with the lid and turn the slow cooker on to its low setting. Cook for 2hr 30min without uncovering, until the sponge feels firm when pressed. Uncover and cook for a further 20min. Dust with icing sugar and serve immediately with cream or ice cream.

Nutritional Value (Amount per Serving):

Calories: 470; Fat: 21.49; Carb: 62.55; Protein: 7.13

Slow-Cooked Gingered Pears

Prep Time: 35 Minutes Cook Time: 4 Hours Serves: 6

Ingredients:

- 1/2 cup finely chopped crystallized ginger
- 1/4 cup packed brown sugar
- 1/4 cup chopped pecans
- 1-1/2 teaspoons grated lemon zest
- 6 medium Bartlett or Anjou pears

- 2 tablespoons butter, cubed
- Optional: Vanilla ice cream and caramel ice cream topping

Directions:

1. In a small bowl, combine the ginger, brown sugar, pecans and zest.
2. Using a melon baller or long-handled spoon, core pears to within 1/4 in. of bottom. Spoon ginger mixture into the center of each pear.
3. Place pears upright in a slow cooker. Top each with butter. Cover and cook on low for 4-5 hours or until tender. If desired, serve with ice cream and caramel topping.

Nutritional Value (Amount per Serving):

Calories: 217; Fat: 7.27; Carb: 37.66; Protein: 1.28

Slow Cooker Mocha Pots de Crème

Prep Time: 15 Minutes Cook Time: 2 Hours Serves: 6

Ingredients:

- 2 cups heavy cream
- 1/2 cup whole milk
- 1/2 cup granulated sugar
- 2 tsp instant coffee or espresso powder
- 6 oz semisweet chocolate, chopped
- 6 large egg yolks
- 2 tsp vanilla extract
- Whipped cream and chocolate shavings for garnish (optional)

Directions:

1. In a saucepan, combine heavy cream, whole milk, granulated sugar, and instant coffee or espresso powder. Heat over medium heat, stirring until the mixture is hot but not boiling.
2. Remove from heat and add the chopped semisweet chocolate. Stir until the chocolate is melted and the mixture is smooth.
3. In a separate bowl, whisk the egg yolks and vanilla extract.
4. Gradually whisk the chocolate mixture into the egg yolks.
5. Strain the mixture to remove any lumps, then pour it into the crock pot.
6. Cover and cook on low for 2 hours or until the pots de crème are set but slightly wobbly in the center.
7. Let them cool to room temperature, then refrigerate until chilled.
8. Garnish with whipped cream and chocolate shavings if desired.

Nutritional Value (Amount per Serving):

Calories: 397; Fat: 27.46; Carb: 31.86; Protein: 5.44

Amaretto Cherries with Dumplings

Prep Time: 15 Minutes Cook Time: 7 Hours 45 Minutes Serves: 6

Ingredients:

- 2 cans (14-1/2 ounces each) pitted tart cherries
- 3/4 cup sugar
- 1/4 cup cornstarch
- 1/8 teaspoon salt
- 1/4 cup amaretto or 1/2 teaspoon almond extract
- 1 cup all-purpose flour
- 1/4 cup sugar
- 1 teaspoon baking powder
- 1/2 teaspoon grated lemon zest
- 1/8 teaspoon salt
- 1/3 cup 2% milk
- 3 tablespoons butter, melted
- Vanilla ice cream, optional

Directions:

1. Drain cherries, reserving 1/4 cup juice. Place cherries in a slow cooker.
2. In a small bowl, mix sugar, cornstarch and salt; stir in reserved juice until smooth. Stir into cherries. Cook, covered, on high for 7 hours. Drizzle amaretto over cherry mixture.
3. For dumplings, in a small bowl, whisk flour, sugar, baking powder, lemon zest and salt. In another bowl, whisk milk and melted butter. Add to flour mixture; stir just until moistened.
4. Drop by tablespoonfuls on top of hot cherry mixture. Cook, covered, 45 minutes or until a toothpick inserted in center of dumplings comes out clean. If desired, serve warm, with ice cream.

Nutritional Value (Amount per Serving):

Calories: 278; Fat: 6.72; Carb: 52.28; Protein: 3.9

APPENDIX RECIPE INDEX

Made in the USA
Las Vegas, NV
19 November 2024